Tokens *of* Courage

Joyce T. Williams

MARIGOLD
PRESS

Published in Savannah, Georgia by Marigold Press Books.
Marigold Press Books titles may be purchased in bulk for educational, business, fundraising, or sales promotional use. For information, please email marigoldpressbooks@gmail.com

Author: Williams, Joyce
Title: Tokens of Courage
ISBN: 979-8-9918316-9-7
Library of Congress Control Number: 2025908335

Cover Design: Jodi Caggige
Book Design: Russ Davis, Bravo Book Designn

To my amazing husband, Bryan, who walked with me and held my hand through it all with unwavering love, support and encouragement.

To Leona and Sage, my beautiful girls, who together served as my compass throughout the storm.

To Mom and Dad, for their endless love and support.

To my brother, Mike, his family; and Linda, Thacker, Jessica & Sarah and theirs. I couldn't have done it without you.

To my therapist, who helped me navigate through my emotional pain; and to all the amazing surgeons, physicians, and nurses who collectively saved my life.

To all my friends and family, let's always remember to rise up again after we fall.

Contents

Introduction

I have a hat that reads: "Life is Good," but sometimes… *sometimes* life seems unnecessarily harsh and cruel. Make no mistake, we may own and support the "Life is Good" outlook; I sure do! But that doesn't mean that we will never fall, never bleed, and never feel the heartache and pain inflicted by our stumbles.

Okay, who am I kidding here… *sometimes* those 'stumbles' feel more like earthquakes that ripple the earth beneath our feet, destroying the foundation we've known and relied on for years until we crumble into the wreckage. *Sometimes* the falls are so painful we are left unable to experience the safety we once knew or even recognize our own reflection in the mirror. *Sometimes* we are left with more questions than answers: *What happened to me? And who will I become?*

Breast cancer is one of those falls. It can be the birthplace of incredible growth and enlightenment, but if you're anything like me, you may want to smack the person who first tells you this, especially if you're in the middle of it. It's not that they're wrong…we can and we will sculpt goodness from our shadows. But we are human and *sometimes* there can be so much pain in a fall that it feels impossible to find your feet again. You can and you will, but give yourself permission to be human and feel that unpleasant thud in the first place. Experiencing the thud does not make you weak!

I've walked this arduous path myself; I've fallen terribly, and I know the thud all too well. It *is* unpleasant.

Still, there is hope.

I'm here to tell you that courage will be the crutches that help you rise each and every time, and here's the beautiful part: courage is *not* saved for a select few. It belongs to every single one of us. We all have it nestled inside of us; we just have to uncover its pieces bit by bit and put it together like a puzzle.

When I was first diagnosed with breast cancer, I felt like I had stepped onto this rickety old raft that had to sail me across a sea of uncertainty. The sky-scraping swells were daunting, the clouds were dark and ominous, and I wasn't sure I would survive the voyage. There was fear. A lot of fear. I knew I wanted to be brave, but courage wasn't something I thought I possessed. As my breast cancer journey took me deeper into the battlefield, I uncovered the courage in my heart one tiny little sliver at a time; and you can find it too.

So, when life begins to stink worse than tuna fish left in the hot sun—and I promise you, whether it's a cancer diagnosis or not, that *stink* will happen to every single one of us at some point—know this: You are stronger and more capable of rising up again than you have ever thought possible! Let's find your fortitude. Let's discover these *Tokens of Courage* housed within your own being, and let their collection help you rise again.

Be mindful, however, that rising doesn't carve off the heartache in the process. It may become part of you, part of your story, but it doesn't have to define you either.

I like to think of this in terms of cookie dough because *that's* a delicious metaphor I can get behind! We are defined neither by the icky, sticky egg nor the sweet, delicious, chocolatey morsels alone; we are the *entire* cookie dough batter—which is pretty damn awesome! The same holds true with our negative experiences and emotions. Our falls and heartaches may be part of our stories, but they're not the whole batter! As much as we may despise our icky sticky eggs, they are part of what makes us whole.

Since information is meant to empower us, and since you can't really talk about rising strong without truly feeling the fall in the first place, I'm going to lay it all out there for you in this book.

In each chapter, I will weave together three threads. First, a *Nugget of Knowledge* to inform and empower us with education. Educating ourselves helps us make informed decisions, know what questions to ask, and focus on something we can actually control during a process. These *Nuggets of Knowledge* I've gathered from interviews with experts, from my biology education at Furman, from the research and curriculum I created on resilience, from formal IRB (Institutional Review Board) studies done with my colleague and friend, Dr. Beth Counselman-Carpenter, as well as from my own lived experiences. These *Nuggets* arm us with a basic understanding of the biology that accompanies a diagnosis, the science of treatments, ways to prepare, how the brain processes trauma, and more. Why? Because knowledge empowers us to better weather our storms!

Woven alongside the education piece will be my *Personal Voyage*—the story of my own journey with breast cancer. It was in this journey where I discovered a powerful way to unlock my own courage. While it sounds heroic, the truth is that sometimes sifting through the rubble of my negative emotions was what allowed me to discover how and where courage could be found.

If courage is a picture of a completed puzzle, the *Tokens of Courage* I learned along the way were the puzzle pieces themselves. I believe when you find them for yourself and piece them together, you will also hold your own courage. These *Tokens of Courage* will make up the last part of each chapter and empower you even further.

I share these *Nuggets of Knowledge*, *Personal Voyages*, and *Tokens of Courage* to arm you—to better equip you. So be proactive, arm yourself with education, know that you're not alone, harness your courage, and RISE AGAIN AFTER BREAST CANCER!

Chapter 1

The Backdrop

Nugget of Knowledge

"Mrs. Williams, when will I ever use this in my life?" my biology students would often inquire. To be candid: the *study* of life may one day in fact *save* your life—it saved mine! Now, isn't that worth learning? Biology, you see, is not a subject saved for the aspiring medic alone. Having a basic understanding of these critical subject areas can prove beneficial for us all.

Cancer is the uncontrollable growth of cells. When a normal cell gets old and wonky, the cell receives a message saying that its services are no longer needed and that it can die off. Cancer happens when those old-wonky cells never receive the self-destruct message, and they *don't* die off. Rather, they continue to divide and form a cluster of old-wonky cells that soon invades healthy tissue nearby. *That* is cancer, and it can be deadly.

So, what exactly prevents this 'self-destruct' message from reaching the old-wonkies in the first place? This question is being continuously studied, and although there is still much to learn, we do know a handful of truths. The inability to deliver the "thank you for your services, we no longer need you, now die-off" message results from some mistake in our DNA. These mistakes (mutations) can be acquired during someone's lifetime or, in some cases, mutations can be inherited.

Your DNA (deoxyribonucleic acid—which is so much fun to say) contains the codes for everything about you. It's the blueprint for who you are. The Human Genome Project, which was completed in 2000, mapped out the entire human genome sequence. Base pairs (adenine, thymine, cytosine, and guanine) combine in a particular order to make up your DNA; a sequence of your DNA is a gene; DNA combined with proteins make up chromosomes (cute little bowtie looking things); and twenty-three pairs of chromosomes (forty-six total) make up a human being.

There are certain genes that scientists know suppress tumors. Translation: These tumor suppressor genes prevent cancer from growing because they are responsible for delivering the self-destruct message to the old-wonkies. If a tumor suppressor gene breaks, either in an individual's lifetime or through inheriting a broken tumor suppressor gene, that person is more susceptible to developing cancer.

Epigenetics is a field of biology where they study the interaction between DNA and proteins to figure out what causes some genes to get turned on and others to get turned off. Would you believe that every somatic cell in your body (every cell but the egg/sperm) has the same DNA: *your* DNA. However, the way your blood cells look and function is vastly different than say, your skin cells or your neurons. *Why? How?* Well, they have the same DNA, but skin cells have skin cell jobs turned on and blood cell jobs turned off.

Metaphorically speaking, the human genome may be the blueprint for your house, but the human *epigenome* explains which lights in the house are turned on and when. Epigentics can play a role in diseases like cancer too. What turns these tumor suppressor genes on or off? The international Human Epigenome Project attempts to help better understand this phenomenon. Factors that may affect what lights are on or off in the house can include environmental factors, medicines, aging, diet, and so forth.

Still, scientists are keenly aware of some hereditary cancer mutations, those passed down from one generation to the next. Most inherited cases of breast cancer are associated with the BRCA1 mutation (which is on chromosome seventeen) and the BRCA2 mutation (which is on chromosome thirteen); however, there are others.

There is an important correction to our colloquialisms about these mutations that ought to be noted. When someone says, "I have the BRCA gene," what they mean to say is they have a *mutation* in their BRCA gene. Everybody has the BRCA genes. They are among those tumor suppressor genes whose job is to deliver the self-destruct message to those old-wonky cells. You *want* those BRCA genes; and you *want* those genes to be working properly. If someone has a mutation in their BRCA gene, then theirs is more or less broken and may fail to deliver that pertinent message to the old-wonky cells; thus cancer can develop.

Most people recognize that if they have a family history of breast cancer, there may be something going on with their genes. However, there's more to know. Let's take a look at chromosomal inheritance. You get half of your genes from your mom and the other half from your dad, so you have forty-six chromosomes (twenty-three pairs).

Your sex chromosomes are chromosome pair number twenty-three. This is what determines if you are a male (XY) or female (XX). It is extremely important to note that the BRCA mutations ARE NOT ON THESE SEX CHROMOSOMES.

The mutation is not on that twenty-third pair. So, the mutation can be inherited from *either* one's mother OR father.

Did you catch that? *Tap, Tap, Tap…pay attention!* The breast cancer hereditary mutations can be inherited from one's father! What if *he* inherited it from his father? Who got it from *his* father? Are you following? The mutation could have been passed down the paternal line and gone undetected for generations!

Everybody knows that early detection saves lives; that's no secret. Breast cancer caught early is easily treated and cured. However, *when* should women pay attention? And *who* really needs to be vigilant? You must arm yourself with knowledge. Understand biology. Know what is normal for you. Ask questions and be proactive.

Personal Voyage

I was a young, suburban mother of two, years away from the recommended surveillance for breast cancer. I didn't have any family history of the disease, and I didn't feel a lump either. For all my doctors and I knew, I was at "average risk." My affinity for genetics coupled with a family history for colon cancer prompted me to consider genetic testing. I had no need to be concerned with breast cancer, none at all. I was an average young mother in her mid-thirties at average risk according to all guidelines.

In August of 2016, I went for my annual OBGYN exam, and as I sat in the waiting room, I was instructed to complete a questionnaire about my family history of cancer. *Wait…who exactly had what? And when?* I needed to write this down. The type-A crazy planner in me wanted to create a color-coordinated chart for my appointment happening in say…five minutes. Practical? Probably not, but I hacked away at it anyway.

I wanted to be prepared for this conversation with my doctor. I knew colon cancer was a thing, but who exactly had it, what age, and when? I needed details. Oh hell, I picked up the phone and called my parents to run through the stats. My paternal grandparents, father, and maternal grandmother all had either colon cancer or precancerous colon polyps. Did you hear that? Colon. *Colon…* the other end, people! It was the end far, far away from those girls upstairs.

My doctor and I discussed these trends and agreed that I was a good candidate for genetic testing. It was plausible that the gene mutation for *colon* cancer ran in my family. I was curious (and absolutely fascinated with family history and genetics), so I agreed to do the test. Breast cancer was nothing that I needed to fear; that genetic mutation was just a bonus test. It was part of the packaged deal. Buy one, get one free I suppose. It was like I scored free XM radio with the purchase of a new car. All that was pertinent to me was the colon cancer gene.

A few weeks later, I received a personal phone call from my doctor. My heart was racing. *What if I had this colon cancer gene?* He greeted me and proceeded to enlighten me on my results. I was negative for the colon cancer gene mutation. I breathed a sigh of relief.

But (oh dear heaven…there was a *but*), I was positive for the BRCA2 mutation. *What the fuck?* Where on earth did this BRCA mutation come from? I had serendipitously stumbled upon this discovery; my physician and I were equally astounded.

Here is what BRCA meant for me. I was at an increased

risk for breast and ovarian cancer, and according to my detailed genetic summary, this mutation gifted me an 84% chance of having breast cancer within my lifetime. *How did this happen? What did this mean for me now?*

This discovery called for increased surveillance. My doctor referred me to a genetic counselor, who reviewed my family history—none of which showed *any* signs of this breast cancer mutation. The genetic counselor and I suspected that the gene likely came down the paternal line, which would explain in part why no family history had been noted thus far.

The genetic counselor, my physician, and I all agreed that alternating every six months with mammograms and MRIs would be crucial for my health plan. I was regarded as "clinically significant," courtesy of the BRCA2 mutation; so I had my first mammogram done in late November of 2016.

Young women often have dense breast tissue, which makes it difficult to navigate the area and locate any potential intruders. I was told it's like driving through a snowstorm. Your windshield wipers may be on turbo, but you still don't see anything. I was no exception, and my mammogram was 'clear.' They were unable to detect the hidden mutants growing within me. I wouldn't discover them until six months later.

Token of Courage: Facts are Friends

When you're swimming outdoors in the summer and thunder rumbles in the distance and clouds begin to condense, do you ignore it and swim blindly, or do you check the weather app instead? Hopefully, you gather the information needed to properly assess the situation and make a sound decision. What are the risks? What are the rewards?

Information is meant to empower us, not cripple us; or as a friend of mine put it so eloquently, "Ignorance is NOT bliss." If we were to plug our ears, close our eyes, and sing: *Nah nah nah nah nah…you can't hurt me*, that wouldn't make whatever it is that's out there less ominous. It would only make us ill-equipped and unprepared to confront it, when and if it does arrive.

So, for the first *Token of Courage*: Gather your data, educate yourself, and be familiar with your own body. Do your mammograms; know your family history; talk with your providers. Fight for your own health! Be vigilant. *You* are your number one advocate, and don't let anyone deter you from that. Ask questions. Be proactive. Don't take no for an answer; and God forbid you find yourself sitting across the table from a doctor confirming your worst nightmare, "You have cancer," then ask even more questions. Gather more data. *What kind of breast cancer? What are my treatment options? What are their risks and their rewards?*

Chapter 2

Into the Unknown

Nugget of Knowledge

My brother and my two little girls each have a 50% chance of having the BRCA2 mutation. The question becomes, should they also do genetic testing? I wish it was a clear-cut answer. Unfortunately, the way the laws are currently written makes it a bit tricky.

My cousin, after having heard my story, was motivated to do genetic testing for herself, and she found out that if you do the testing and are positive for one of these mutations, you could be denied life insurance. Although you couldn't be denied health insurance, life insurance was a completely different story. I re-evaluated my situation. *Would this have changed things for me? Should I have not done the testing?* For me, had I not done the testing, I would have died.

If my brother does the testing and is negative for the mutation, then his little girls don't need to worry. However, if he is positive for the BRCA2 mutation, he could be denied life insurance. What then? Do you recommend testing?

Furthermore, I was also told that you cannot do this genetic testing on a minor. Many people have asked me if I will encourage my two girls to do the testing. Honestly, it will depend on how the laws are written as my children become of age. Yes, knowledge is power, and I would want them to know. However, my current understanding of the law, as explained to me by the genetic counselor, is that insurance will have to cover my girls' mammograms and MRIs ten years prior to my age of diagnosis.

So, they can begin their surveillance way before age 40 (they don't need genetic testing for that; they can use me and my experiences as reason enough). If, however, they do genetic testing and are positive for the mutation, they too could be denied life insurance; but if they are negative, they are put into the general population's risk category and have to wait until 40 for a baseline.

Personal Voyage

A mere six months after my initial mammogram, in early June of 2017, I went in for my very first MRI screening. Only then were my cancer masses discovered. Yep, masses...plural. I was 36 years old, and I had three masses in one breast. I actually *had* cancer...*breast* cancer. *How did this happen?*

Early summer was approaching, and we were all getting excited for school to be out. We had visions of long days at the beach, picnicking by the pool, late family movie nights, and perhaps a trip or two. I could almost smell the mixture of sweat, coconut, and sunblock. Bring on the relaxation and sunshine! Grab me a margarita, play me some Jimmy Buffet, and throw in the smell of a barbeque on the patio. I just had to make it through a routine check-up first, and then it would be play time.

After the accidental BRCA2 discovery, we were doing aggressive surveillance with mammograms and MRIs alternating every six months. This was no big deal; we were just being extra attentive. I had always been proactive. I liked to be prepared, organized, and plan for the future, so when doctors enlightened me of my unrealized gene, I wanted nothing more than to monitor things closely.

My mammogram in November didn't show anything, so I wasn't too worried about the MRI. The biggest scare for me at the time was crawling into that tube and feeling trapped. I wasn't claustrophobic; but I despised feeling confined all the same.

My second stressor stemmed from the fact that I was a people-pleaser down to the core. It was likely etched into my bones, stamped deep within my marrow: *never, ever, ever make anyone feel put-out, inconvenienced, or feel bad if they're unable to help you…ergo, never be a burden.* By extension, I rationalized: *If I never ask for help, I can avoid that risk.* The very thought of inconveniencing another sent my anxiety through the roof. *I couldn't ask; I shouldn't ask.* I feared asking for help in any capacity would brand me as that burden I vowed never to be.

Yet, this appointment came at a time where I needed backup. I needed a trusted friend to watch my girls while I made the trek to town for the MRI; I couldn't take them with me, and I needed to go. Surrendering to the idea that I couldn't do everything on my own was one of the first challenges of many to come.

I wish I could go back in time and pat that poor, frazzled version of myself on the back and somehow convince her that *it is* OKAY! We're all human, and we ALL need help from time to time. However, at this point in my life I tortured myself whenever I had to ask anything of anybody. I not only agonized over when and how to ask a friend to watch my kids that day; but since nobody was allowed in the room with me during the

MRI, I also told my husband, Bryan, not to worry about leaving work. I'd make the trip by myself.

I felt both heroic and stupid for going there alone. I felt strength in handling my own business, yet foolish for having placed myself into emotional goop without reinforcements or back-up of any kind. I had to lay face down on a sliding table that went into a panic-inducing tube, and I had to remain perfectly still.

Soon, tears dripped down my cheeks and landed on the table beneath me. My nose started to get stuffy, and it was hard to breathe with my anxiety on the rise. *Great! Don't move, Joyce! Lay perfectly still or you'll screw this up and have to do another.* Still, calming down was much easier said than done, especially when the tears began to interfere with inhaling and exhaling like a normal person.

When it was finally over, and I was released from the confining tube, I darted towards my car to make the trip home in hopes of beating rush hour traffic. I wanted to make it back to town to get my kids before dinner time. (Okay, to be honest, I wanted to get my kids before I had overstayed my welcome and morphed into the dreaded burden that I feared so much.) At least I was done for now; free for another year before having to endure another MRI.

Two days later, one of my best friends, Michelle, and I had taken the kids to the playground. It was a gorgeous day, perfect for being outside. She and I sat and talked at the picnic tables while the girls ran around and climbed on the monkey bars. My phone rang, and it was a number I didn't recognize, so I let it go to voicemail. As soon as I did, I realized that it could have been the doctor's office. *Shit. I should have answered it. What was I thinking?* My voicemail notification soon dinged, and I quickly dialed in my codes to retrieve the mystery message. Sure enough, it was my doctor's office. Oh boy! *Breathe, Joyce.*

I listened to my voicemail and tried to focus on her words while simultaneously listening to the screams and giggles of little girls running around in the background. The nurse left a message to call her back; they had my MRI results and had found three masses on my right breast. *What was I hearing? What was happening?* I couldn't quite think.

She went on to say that the hospital was going to call me shortly to set up an ultrasound appointment in efforts to verify the nature of these masses. *Hang on…another doctor's appointment? Masses?* She told me not to panic just yet; there were lots of false positives read from MRIs. She continued, "They are very sensitive machines." Nevertheless, they wanted to do an ultrasound to know what exactly the images were showing.

Inhale. Exhale. *Wait, what were the steps for breathing again?*

I was in shock. The deer in headlights syndrome fell hard upon my heart. *What did I just hear? There were three masses? Was I dreaming?* I started laughing. *Laughter* is what came out of my body, not tears, not anger… laughter. I told Michelle it wasn't good news, and then I smiled and laughed! Who does that? I didn't know what else to do or how to get a handle on what exactly I was feeling because this just couldn't be true. It was a bad joke somehow. It had to be.

Sure enough, the next day the hospital called to set up an ultrasound. I went by myself to that appointment, too. Emotions were bound to stir, yet I shuffled forward thinking I could will them away.

It was officially summer vacation but certainly not the margarita and Jimmy Buffet version I had envisioned. The kids were out of school, and I had to rely on friends once more in order to deal with these looming appointments. It was excruciating.

As I dragged myself down to Savannah for my ultrasound, I tried to reason the shaky nerves and escalating fear out of my soul. *This wasn't a big deal. These machines were just sensitive, right? This appointment was just a formality, a way to be thorough.* The sonographer and doctor were examining my MRI scan, taking images, and talking with me. I had a hard time focusing on much of what was going on. My mind started to wander: *What if this was serious? Masses? That sounds like a word thrown around when people talk about cancer. I couldn't have cancer. My mammogram was clear. I didn't feel a lump.*

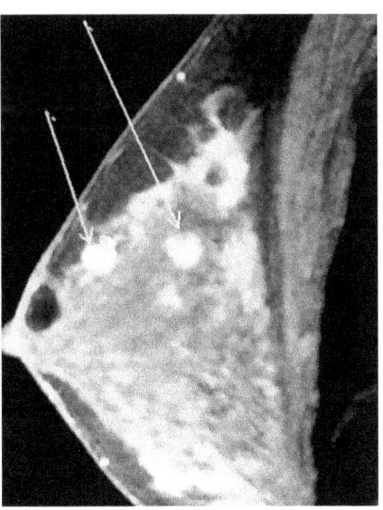

Fig. 1. Joyce's MRI image from June 2017

The doctor wanted to refer me upstairs to the Center for Breast Care where high risk patients were seen. She went on to tell me that these masses were solid, not fluid filled. This meant that they could either be fibroids or cancer, and they needed to order a biopsy to know for sure.

Two days after my ultrasound, I had another appointment to get a biopsy done. Dr. Rehl, the breast surgeon, performed the biopsy. She numbed my breast, and I closed my eyes so as not to see the gigantic cutting devices that approached my body. It didn't hurt too much, but I knew that I'd be bruising later. She sliced through tissue to achieve the correct spot to sample, then *punch, punch, punch!* The miniature cookie cutter stamped out cores of tissue that looked like spaghetti noodles. She took a handful of samples, patched me up, and said she would contact me as soon as she had the results.

Token of Courage: Ask for Help

During this time, I agonized over the prospects of "putting people out" or being "high-maintenance." I wanted to be in-dependent and self-sufficient; and in my mind, asking for help made me feel even further away from those attributes. The more I was strong-armed and forced by my circumstances to ask for help, the harsher I became with myself for needing anything and the more I resented what was happening to me. However, hindsight is a beautiful thing. I have since learned that asking for help does not make you a terrible person. *It makes you a human being.* Better yet, it makes you part of the tribe, part of the village in which you live. *We're not meant to live life alone.* Giving help and allowing yourself to receive it in return are BOTH a part of belonging and being loved.

We have to be willing to embrace our vulnerability and let it be okay that we are not perfect, that we cannot do everything all the time. Superhumans belong in fairy tales. *Real* humans struggle and need help from time to time, and that doesn't negate our strength. Allow yourself to be *real* rather than make-believe.

Initially, when I was told that I had cancer, I aspired to be like Poppy from the hit movie, *Trolls.* I was up against an intimidating hardship but set out on this voyage with unshakable determination and optimism. *I would not let this scary, dark path shake me from what I needed to do in order to live.* Bless my heart. I even pictured myself running through my world of pain with Poppy's infectious smile. Maybe I could even sing a song and dance right out of the troll-eating flower.

Fast forward through the movie, and just like Poppy, I also felt defeated. My optimism and intent to fix things seemed at a loss, and the color drained from my being as sadness and discouragement crept in. I needed to learn to love and accept myself in my entirety: the good, the bad, and the ugly. Only then could I recognize and accept what true beauty was—who *I* really was—but oh, dear God, did I struggle to learn this.

I felt shattered. My spirit, the essence of who I was, had been busted into a thousand shards. There was unbelievable heartache and pain…and my way-less-than-perfect soul was laid bare before me. People pleasing and perfectionism had always been my go-to tactics; I naively thought that if I would only work harder, be stronger, and do just the right things at just the right times, then I could overcome any adversity. It took me a LONG time to throw that rule book out the window and to reckon that it was okay to not always be okay.

Glass mosaics are made, not when you mend the broken pieces, or when you turn back time to recreate what was taken, but when you assemble those pieces into a new, beautiful whole. Although you too may have fallen—and been broken—your own mosaic is captivating and strong; and there is nothing more beautiful than the *you* you are now. You are enough. You don't have to bend, or pretend, or conform. Embrace the mosaic and ask for help.

Mosaic

Once I harbored silver linings
Graffitied them in dungeon's findings
Anywhere there were such tidings
Rainbows shot to shield from night.

Onward with my smiley notion
Oblivious to wicked's potion
Brewing up in secret motion
Optimism reigned the sights.

'Tis the way I marched through darkness
Blissfully blinded to the starkness
Always sunshine left me mark-less
Through the gentle tugs of life.

Once a season came upon me
Pirating life to topsy-turvy
Ripping rugs from underneath me
Colors bled and opened strife

In a world with color fading
Perception was a crooked shading
Slammed me to the floor – no aiding
All Hallow's Eve: pink décor.

Drowning in a sea of hardships
Tsunami's over flooded tight grip
Pleading breathes would find the right trip
To my lungs, I did implore.

Owning scars and skin that crackled
Raggedly trapped in cancer's shackles
Onward marching into tackle
Facing losses large as life.

Trembling through exotic turmoil
Emotional wounds began to boil
Begging cancer's plot to foil
Help me blot this with a knife.

Fumbling for my rainbowed goggles
Still knowing that my shadows squabbled
Masking murals that I'd cobbled
'till the truth unveiled alas.

Then I noticed honest dances
Uncovered eyes soon bore the chances
Ballet between two old stances
Where yin and yang breached across.

Light and darkened all together
Purposely called to then untether
Silver lining's fibbed Mayweather
Since truth, 'they don't define us.'

Banged and bleeding with my grumbles
Wiping the sweat and tears from stumbles
Found my feet despite that crumble
Rise again from broken dust.

Shards of glass had seen me splattered
Resilient rising pieced the shattered
Sculpted out of endless clatter
Born mosaic, now reformed.

Strengthened from my untied blindings
Transformed out of chrysalis bindings
Courage pieced by life unwinding
So, break the rigid rules confining

Know that grace is yours defining
And hear the secret truth confiding
You are not alone residing
And stronger still with pink combining
Together we weather this storm.

Chapter 3

Virginia Gets the Call

Nugget of Knowledge

When diagnosed, it may seem obvious that physical wounds are imminent; however, the emotional trauma hits women unexpectedly. Many do not anticipate the psychological stress involved in a cancer diagnosis, nor are they aware of the emotional healing required to mend completely. Many set off on a mission to get shit done and don't allow themselves to truly feel while in "warrior mode." Some of it is our body's survival mechanism, and it works.

However, navigating a heightened intensity of emotions *will be* just as big a part of the journey as the physical hurdles. Please don't think that you're alone in dealing with it! When you feel those negative emotions, it doesn't mean that you're doing something wrong, and it sure as hell doesn't mean you are weak! It means you are human. It is part of this process; unfortunately, it's an element to this journey that's not publicly talked about nearly enough…yet. Countless women have confided in me this same truth: Dealing with breast cancer is traumatic.

A breast cancer diagnosis and the treatments that follow are indeed life altering. There is fear, anger, sadness, and grief all rolled up together at times. We are human and are bound to feel that inevitable *shake* when something of this magnitude comes trampling in on our lives.

Depression, anxiety, and PTSD (post-traumatic stress disorder) are common. Experiencing these emotions, turning towards them, and acknowledging them does NOT equate to weakness. In fact, it is quite brave to face them, learn to accept them, ask for help, and experience self-growth. *How the hell do you do that?* It takes time, and honestly, the willingness to work with a licensed therapist to help you gain perspective and reframe your thoughts can be invaluable in the process.

Radical Acceptance is part of Dialectical Behavior Therapy (DBT); it is essentially recognizing that you can accept these events and emotions as part of your story without giving into them and letting them define you. Acceptance does not mean that you are okay with it. Good or bad: You see it, you acknowledge it, you learn from it, and you grow.

Cognitive Behavioral Therapy (CBT) is used to help clients recognize patterns of negative thinking so they can alter their strategies for facing challenges in a healthier way. EMDR (eye movement desensitization and reprocessing) is a kind of psychotherapy that has been used to treat trauma and PTSD. It involves recalling the traumatic event while a therapist uses bilateral stimulation (following a light or finger moving while readdressing your trauma). The idea is that it acts like the processing that we're able to do in REM sleep, thus helping our brains integrate our traumatic memories. Some therapists use several of these modalities together to help cancer patients recover and find their way forward after treatment.

Personal Voyage

After my biopsy, my brother, Mike, who was in the Army, was preparing to PCS (Permanent Change of Station) again. He had been stationed in Maryland for the past three years and had received orders for his next assignment to Germany. He and his family packed up and shipped off their home goods, put their house on the market, and moved in with my parents in Virginia for a few weeks prior to their flight overseas. While they were there, Bryan and I wanted to bring our two daughters, Leona (age 5) and Sage (age 4), up so that we could all visit prior to my brother's move. It would likely be three years before we would see them again, so this was a trip I didn't want to miss!

Upon our arrival, the whole clan (Mike, Stephanie, their three girls, and my parents) met us in the driveway armed with nearly three hundred water balloons! We barely exited the car after an eight and a half hour drive before my brother launched the first one in my direction. *Oh, it was on, big brother!* The eleven of us engaged in a gigantic

Fig. 2. Family photo in Virginia June of 2017

water balloon war. There were no teams, it was every man for himself, and when we ran out of balloons, my big brother introduced me to the newest tactic: dump the bucket of cold water over my head. We were all drenched! This was the first of many water balloon battles to be had on this trip. There was never a safe time; if you were outside, you were fair game. People were attacked coming home with groceries, while up on the deck playing, early in the morning, while cooking dinner outside, in the evenings after the kids had baths. It didn't matter. Sometimes we had to change clothes four or five times a day! But we laughed until our sides hurt. We ran, we hid, and every single one of us tapped into our inner child and played hard. And when we had become the target of a surprise launch and found ourselves dripping from head to toe for the fifth time in a day, we plotted our revenge with a grin.

I was glad to be home, to be with my family. I was distracted and at times could forget about the agony of waiting for a call about my biopsy results. I had it in my head that the call would come on Monday, which was the day that we all took a trip to Kings Dominion. The amusement park had a new roller coaster since we'd been there last, and Mike was insistent that his little sister muster up some courage and ride it with him.

Oh, hell, live a little Joyce! We went to ride the Intimidator 305, which was the tallest roller coaster on the East Coast. The first drop was from three hundred feet in the air at a nearly 85-degree angle. Although there were no loops, the twists and turns at 90 mph speed had me suspended in the air. I couldn't get my butt to stay on the chair; thank God for harnesses! I cursed at Mike as the coaster kept climbing that initial height, and I may or may not have punched him after it was over. He, of course, did the big brother laugh.

We spent the rest of the day riding coasters after coasters, taking turns with the kids on their rides, eating funnel cakes, and having a ball. By the time the late afternoon thunderstorm started to roll in, we were all exhausted and ready to head out.

It was good that we went to Kings Dominion that day. I was anticipating that phone call, but it never came. I checked my phone regularly for missed calls, but there were none. It was good that I was otherwise distracted. Looking back on this moment, I am grateful the phone call had waited. I was gifted this day. I was given the opportunity to fly through the hills at mach speed, be scared right out of my pants, and then feel the earth beneath my feet again. I can say, looking back, that this roller coaster moment mirrored my journey to come. There were highs, lows, and true terror; but I held on through my fear and came out afterwards with solid ground beneath my feet again.

The next morning, we left the kids with their dads, and Mom, Steph, and I went down the road to Target for a bit. We were perusing the little girl's clothes, picking out shirts for each of them when my phone rang. I recognized the number right away; this was it. "I need to take this," I said, answered the phone, and began to walk outside.

"Hello?" I answered, my voice already shaky.

"Hello, Joyce. This is Dr. Rehl." Her voice sounded neutral, and I was too nervous to read anything into it.

"Hi, Dr. Rehl. So…is it good news or bad news?" I thought if I asked the question casually, then perhaps it would lessen the gravity of what was happening. For a microsecond I played out her response in my head, something to the effect of: *No worries, all is well.* However, her voice responded for real on the other line, and she said,

"I'm afraid that it is bad news. It is cancer."

As I reached the red bench outside and sat down, my world came crashing down around me. I was alone on the phone with a doctor who just told me that something that kills people was growing inside of me…ME! *Was I going to die? I didn't want to die!*

Tears flooded the corners of my eyes until I finally blinked and sent them chasing one another down my cheeks. I was trying to stay focused and level-headed, keeping my emotional responses at bay so I could grasp everything she was telling me. However, I wasn't doing a great job. I was heartbroken; I was broken. I was collapsing on the inside, emotionally falling to pieces.

She told me to meet with her next week when I returned back home to discuss treatment options, but they were going to need to do surgery: a mastectomy. She told me to try not to worry too much; what I had was "treatable and curable." She also advised me to stay off of the internet until she went over the exact kind of cancer I had. Apparently, there were multiple varieties of breast cancer. Prior to this moment in my life, I had no idea.

I hung up the phone after making our appointment and went back into Target. Mom and Steph were waiting for me at the entrance just past the dollar section. There was no hiding it. They could tell from my face what the news was. I gave my mom a huge hug as I cried and told her that I had cancer.

Stephanie and I went to the car while Mom went to pay for the shirts. After a few minutes, Mom came out, and the three of us sat there for a few minutes letting it soak in. We talked about how far medicine had come and what they could do now with surgeries and reconstruction. We talked about how we'd figure this out. Somehow.

Then we gathered ourselves together and set out to get some fast food to bring back for everyone. I needed to talk to Bryan. He and I gathered our food and had a picnic in the side garden. There were no water balloons now; there was no chasing and laughing and merriment to hide behind. It was just he and I sitting alongside this bombshell. The news hit him like a Mack truck too; while I cried, he got angry. *This could not be happening to his wife!*

It was going to take some time to process for both of us, and neither of us knew exactly how to do it. I began to fill my time with embracing distractions and coaching my determination. I *would* solve this problem. Step one: Meet with the surgeon. Step two: Have surgery. In the interim, I focused on family, water balloon wars, and anything else to keep my mind and body busy. Okay, there were a handful of margaritas and chocolate chip cookies too. When I needed a minute, I'd escape up to my room, cry a little, and then wash my face and head back to any distraction I could find. Bryan, on the other hand, plunged himself into research mode.

Token of Courage: Let Go of What You Can't Control

I used to think that therapy was great for *other* people, but I, myself, would *never* need to go. *Oh boy! How terribly wrong was I?* Emotions are deeply human. Learning to understand your personal coping skills and additional techniques is more powerful than you can ever imagine! It has absolutely nothing to do with being *less than*; rather, it has everything to do with setting yourself up for optimal success—no matter who you are or what your story is.

As a teacher, I was a huge advocate for helping my students discover *how* they learned. If they could first understand their metacognition, then they would better grasp the concepts I was trying to teach, because everyone learns differently. I would administer a test to determine their preferred method of learning, and then I modeled and practiced different note taking and studying techniques that appealed to each of the different modalities of learning. After that, students could choose what method worked best for them. Learning could happen best once they knew *how* they learned.

Similarly, healing emotionally can happen when you explore ways to process and settle on the strategies that work best for you. *Everyone* can benefit from going to therapy. Going to therapy simply means that you're taking an active role in learning more about yourself so that you can truly heal, grow from your experiences, and become more equipped to handle adversity in both the present and the future. In essence, these safe, non-judgmental spaces where you unload and process through life with a trained professional actually help with your post-traumatic growth.

Therapy became a life raft for me. Still, I kept this confession, this admission of needing help, of seeing a professional, heavily guarded in the beginning. Perfectionism, after all, still had its claws deep into my flesh, and the idea of admitting that I didn't always have things together sent my insides wanting to run for the hills. I am the biggest control freak known to man. The lack of control in my life bothered me immensely as I moved forward into my storm. The reality was: I *didn't* have control over so many things. For me, this was earth-shattering and, quite frankly, *terrifying*.

Over and over my therapist, Ashley, would tell me that I needed to let go of the things I couldn't control and focus on the things I could. I swear I tried. In theory, I knew of its power and aimed to adopt this outlook, but at the ground level, I continued struggling with this shift in perspective and in being able to actually let go. However, one day the stars were aligned just right, I was in a place where I could better hear this, and Ashley spoke using language that clicked with me.

Ashley compared life to a roller coaster: ups and downs along the way. That part of the metaphor is nothing earth-shattering or new, but here's where it became more powerful and life altering. In regards to control, she said to think about a roller-coaster rider. She said there were two ways to experience the ride. You could 'white-knuckle-it' and try to control the ups, downs, and loops, or you could raise your arms in the air and let go of the illusion of control. Both are on the ride; both are scared, but their experiences of the journey are vastly different.

It took me a year before I grasped this revelation, but it seems appropriate to mention it now in light of my Kings Dominion trip. I survived the Intimidator 305 with my brother. I *was* scared. I faced the ups and downs, and I was absolutely certain my harness would fail and I would fly off and plummet to the ground at any given point. However, it was only a stop along the way in the entirety of the park. It was a part of my day, but it was not my entire day. Soon, I felt safe on the solid ground once more.

The third token to finding courage is plain and simple, folks: Let go of the things that you can't control and focus your attention on the things you can. You may not be able to control the fact that you have cancer or that the doctors aren't calling you the second you will your phone to ring. You may not be able to control what treatment plans are recommended or when, but take ownership of those small things that you can control. When you're first diagnosed, and it feels like the weight of the world is hijacking your life and suffocating you in the process… when it feels like BIG, SCARY THINGS are happening to you and you can't control any of them, focus on what you *can* do. As soon as you're diagnosed, find somebody to talk to, carve time out of your schedule, and set up that safe, processing space. It is much easier to find that space in the beginning than it is to search for it in the midst of the storm.

Chapter 4

Survival Strategy

Nugget of Knowledge

I used to think that cancer was simply defined based on where it was found in the body. Lung cancer was cancer in the lungs; colon cancer was cancer in the colon; *breast* cancer was cancer found in the breast. Little did I know there were several kinds of breast cancer.

It's like going to buy toothpaste; there are countless different brands, and within each brand there are about thirty different subcategories. Cancer, I've come to learn, is a word that operates much the same way. There are many different flavors of breast cancer, and their treatments differ accordingly.

There are a series of ducts in the breast that connect milk producing glands, called lobules, to the nipple. Breast cancer can originate in either the lobules or the ducts, and if the cancer stays confined to its origination site, then it is called *in situ*. However, if the cancer has eaten a hole through its initial site and begun to leak into surrounding breast tissue, it is referred to as *invasive*. Invasive ductal carcinoma would therefore be cancer that originated in the milk ducts but has broken free into the surrounding breast tissue. Furthermore, Inflammatory Breast Cancer (IBC) does not involve a lump at all.

The stage of your cancer, stage one, two, three or four, is based on a series of criteria including the cancer's size, location, lymph node involvement, and whether or not it has metastasized. If breast cancer reaches the lymph nodes and travels, or metastasizes to your bones, that is not bone cancer. Rather, it is stage four metastatic breast cancer.

If a tumor is estrogen and progesterone positive, then doctors may recommend hormone inhibitors. Similarly, if a patient's breast cancer is HER2 positive (which refers to a protein), doctors have another layer of treatment that they can offer: Herceptin. If you hear of triple negative breast cancer being difficult to treat, that is because the patient's cancer is negative for both the hormone receptors and HER2. Consequently, the patient would not be a candidate for hormone blockers or Herceptin.

Personal Voyage

Bryan and I met with Dr. Rehl on the 28th of June to review my biopsy results in detail. Not that this news wasn't *real* before, but something about being gifted a bright orange, two-inch binder stamped with "Cancer Institute" filled with copious amounts of cancer information cemented the gravity of it all. The anxiety building while waiting for the doctor to arrive coupled with that orange binder resting on the countertop were like weights pinning us somewhere between denial and fear. I, of course, cried; Bryan got angry. I *hated* this exam room.

My surgeon reviewed the details on my type of breast cancer as well as our treatment options, and we had numerous questions. She told us that I had invasive ductal carcinoma: cancer that originated inside the milk ducts but had breached the wall of the duct and started to eat through normal breast tissue. It was the story of *The Great Cancer Escape*; my body was writing its own damn book and didn't bother to consult me.

She told us the tumor was estrogen and progesterone positive; in other words, those hormones fed it. *Did birth control feed it? Was my own body killing me by whipping up hormone food for cancer cells?* Dr. Rehl assured me this was good because it meant that my tumor would respond well to treatment.

I was also HER2 negative, which I was clueless about at the time. At that moment, I didn't really care. I couldn't *unhear* the word cancer. It was on a continuous loop playing in my head, and I struggled hearing anything else. *You have cancer. People die of cancer. You need surgery to remove the cancer. Cancer. Cancer. Cancer. Orange binder about your cancer.* All my brain could filter at the time was cancer, so when I heard that estrogen and progesterone positive cancers could be more easily treated, I stopped listening. I still couldn't smudge out and erase the word *cancer.* I was still hung up on those six little letters.

I had three masses in my right breast, of which one was biopsied. It was 1.2 cm in size, about the size of a pea. My cancer was currently described as stage 1B, although they also gave the cells a grade based on how crazy their nuclei looked in comparison to normal breast cells. Mine was a two to three score, which meant they were pretty freaking wonky. *Fantastic! The mutant cells have escaped, and God only knows where they're traveling.* Positive vs negative, I didn't give a damn. *Get it out of me!* This was more or less the treatment plan.

I needed surgery, and I needed it soon. Having either a lumpectomy or a mastectomy was discussed. However, there was no way she would have been able to remove all three masses and have much of a breast left. Moreover, I was positive for the BRCA2 mutation, and my body had proved itself worthy of the mutation's reputation. With all things considered, a lumpectomy was not an option.

They would have to remove the entire breast, nipple included, since the cancer was too close to leave a safe enough margin. The only choice to be made was whether or not they would take both of my breasts or just the one. When I asked what the likelihood was of my left breast having or getting cancer, she told us the chances of me having it were low, but my chances of getting it were still at 84% (thank you, BRCA2 mutation).

She said they would also perform a sentinel node biopsy during surgery. This meant they would inject a radioactive dye to ascertain which lymph nodes were in jeopardy. Then, she would remove those nodes during surgery and have them biopsied as well. I knew it was bad if the cells reached the lymph nodes, *so yes please check and make sure that they didn't get to that train station and hop a ride to some unknown destination in my body: brain, liver, bone, ovaries. Cut it out and do it before those mutant cells decide to travel!*

She reviewed parts of the surgery, my hospital stay, and my recovery. She also referred me to a plastic surgeon, Dr. Pearl. The two surgeons would coordinate their surgery times and operate under the same anesthesia. She would go first and remove the tissue, and then he would follow and insert the expanders, place the drains, and stitch me up. We went ahead and scheduled a consultation with Dr. Pearl as well.

Even though I had already jumped on the "cut it out" wagon, the question was asked, "What is my prognosis if we did nothing?" Dr. Rehl paused, though never breaking eye contact. I could see the wheels turning; she was compassionate and kind and was trying to figure out a way to communicate in a way that was both tender and truthful. She handled it well, but there's no good way to hear that cancer is growing inside of you. No matter what, it just royally sucks. I already knew the answer anyway: *death*. Doing nothing would certainly kill me, and that wasn't an option worth taking.

Token of Courage: Practice Gratitude

Sometimes in life, our greatest nightmares haunt us and cripple us with fear. They find a way to creep into the safety of our room and bind our hands and feet until we feel hopeless, or angry, or overcome with grief. Now, I'm not saying that these emotions don't have their place, nor am I saying that I think that tragedies and traumas are part of the "everything happens for a reason" motto. No!

However, what I am saying is that when life does hit us hard, after taking a moment to inhale and exhale, take a second moment to be grateful. No, you don't need to be grateful that a loved one died, that you lost your job or were diagnosed with a deadly disease. Be grateful in times like these, not that it happened, but for what else you have going for you around that giant boulder. This helps nurture hope.

Me, for example? I traced my gratefulness all the way back to ninth grade biology. I hated science back then with a passion; but then as fate or luck or a higher power or whatever you want to call it happened, I was placed in a biology class with one of the most amazing teachers of all time. This woman took a kid who *hated* science and flipped things around so much for her that when that kid left her class at the end of the year, she not only loved science but swore she'd become a biology major. And I did.

I'm NOT grateful for my cancer! Hell no! I am, however, *grateful* for my biology teacher. I'm *grateful* that I developed a love for science, specifically biology. I'm *grateful* for my passion for teaching. I'm *grateful* that I became a biology teacher. I'm *grateful* that I taught genetics, that I knew about these genetic mutations, and that I knew enough to ask. I'm *grateful* that my OB had that questionnaire that day. I'm *grateful* that we did the screenings, that I fell into the care of the doctors that I did when I did, and that we found my cancer early. I'm *grateful* for having started therapy when I did, for being home with my family when I found out I had cancer, for having a supportive husband, and for having my children when I did.

Finding ways to be grateful in the midst of something so horrible does not mean that you appreciate the thing that was horrible. But being grateful for the things along the way or in the events that follow is the fourth token to finding courage. Gratefulness and hope take courage; and when you actively look for them, you're undeniably cultivating the growth of more courage.

Chapter 5

Blueprints of a New Body

Nugget of Knowledge

Treatment is highly individualized, because no two cancers are identical, and no two patients' body chemistries are exactly the same. What is recommended for you will be a tailored conversation with your provider based on your own medical needs. Surgery, chemotherapy, radiation, hormone inhibitors, etc…your treatment plan will be individualized. That being said, surgery is often one of these layers of treatment, and depending on individual risk factors and diagnoses, a lumpectomy or a mastectomy can be performed to remove the cancer. A lumpectomy is the removal of part of the breast whereas a mastectomy is the removal of the entire breast tissue.

After a mastectomy is performed, some women choose to have reconstruction done, while others don't. Women who refrain from any sort of reconstruction can opt to either "go flat" or utilize external prosthesis (they make special bras that hold them too). Still, other women prefer some type of reconstruction. Consulting with a plastic surgeon is beneficial, as there are different methodologies of reconstructing the breast. Like always, it will be a personal decision.

Breast reconstruction can involve DIEP (Deep Inferior Epigastric Perforator) flaps or implants. The DIEP flap breast reconstruction involves the removal of healthy tissue, skin, and fat from the patient's lower abdomen and recreating a new breast from that tissue. Alternative flap procedures involve removing tissue from either the buttocks or back.

Another option is reconstruction with implants. Sometimes surgeons will be able to go straight to the implant during a patient's mastectomy surgery, but again it will depend on individual body make up. Otherwise, patients can have expanders inserted at the time of the mastectomy, slowly have them filled up with saline to the desired size, and then have them switched out for silicone implants at a later surgery date.

As far as the nipples go, some women are candidates for nipple sparing. This means that their original nipples can be saved and sewn back in place following a mastectomy. However, not everyone is a candidate for nipple sparing (perhaps if they have a hereditary mutation, or if their cancer was too close in proximity), and still some women choose not to save their nipples regardless. Other options with nipples include nipple reconstruction, 3D nipple tattooing, or deciding to go without them altogether.

Personal Voyage

I spoke with a woman who, as fate would have it, also had the breast cancer mutation *and* had the same breast surgeon and plastic surgeon that I had. This woman also had a bilateral mastectomy followed by reconstruction. What an amazing opportunity: to be able to talk with someone who had already left their footprints on this shaky ground. I was only moments away from having to place my big toe across that terrifying threshold myself, and it was comforting to hear from someone who had been there.

At this point, I had yet to meet with the plastic surgeon, and I was curious for the insider scoop. She told me how pleased she was with the plastic surgeon's work, that he was thorough and attentive, and that he always made her a priority. Well, that was encouraging because my nerves were becoming firecrackers, and I needed all the help that I could get to extinguish them.

Bryan went with me to my consultation appointment, and we were both a little anxious waiting to be seen. I hated myself for being there. I hated the cancer for directing me, for commandeering my body, and orchestrating this whole damn thing! My mind was stuck in a continuous loop in the waiting room: *My physical image is about to be drastically altered.* I didn't want to change my body. I wanted *my* breasts, and I despised that they were about to be taken from me, even though I knew my life depended on it. I craved authenticity and feared I was losing it to cancer. I feared I was losing myself along with the loss of my breasts. However, knowing a mastectomy was imminent, I wanted to feel as close to my pre-surgery self and as close to normal as I could get. So, there I was: dragged in by the ears by cancer, kicking and screaming internally, and wallowing in my own disdain despite knowing that I really wanted boobs—be them mine or prostheses.

We entered the exam room, and I slipped on the robe. I came to love these robes for they welcomed and hugged me, unlike the paper thin, butt-showing hospital gowns. I climbed up on the table and waited for Dr. Pearl to arrive. My anxiety revved up in its intensity; however, when Dr. Pearl entered the room for the very first time, Bryan and I immediately clicked with him. We appreciated, trusted, and valued him immensely; he was kind and supportive. When I started to get a little emotional, he told me it was okay. He also told me that I was fighting cancer, which kind of made me a badass. A smile crept onto my face; I liked him. Bryan liked him too.

Dr. Pearl and his nurse reviewed my reconstruction process. Since I didn't have enough tissue on my abdomen or anywhere else, they would insert the tissue expanders and stitch them in place somewhere underneath the muscle on the top half, and then they would use something called AlloDerm to support the implant on the bottom half.

Dr. Pearl's team would be responsible for putting in the drains. I needed four of them: two on each side; and from what I heard, those things were horrible. I wouldn't be able to shower with them, and my mobility would be limited. Furthermore, I would be leaking blood, fluid, and nasty shit of some sort into these plastic grenade-looking containers and would be responsible for dumping and monitoring the volume of shit that oozed. *Awesome!*

After inserting the expanders and the drains, Dr. Pearl would stitch me up and follow up with me post-surgery. He would likely refrain from putting in any saline during surgery; he would have to see how much tissue I had, and how things looked then. My anxiety grew! I knew what that meant. Without any saline, there would be a period of time when I wouldn't just be flat; I could be *concave*…that unsubstantiated nasty little rumor did laps in my brain. Yet, how could I possibly protest? Cancer would kill me if I didn't move forward. They had to go. My breasts *had* to go.

Eventually, Dr. Pearl would remove the drains. Then, he would begin injecting the expanders with saline until I reached my desired size. The expanders have a magnetic port the size of a quarter that is used after surgery to locate where to insert the saline. *Sweet, at least I would be magnetic! What a cool party trick!* I was desperate to armor up with silver linings and sarcasm. I was scared and wanted strength, so I made jokes and tried to poke the situation for humor when and where I could.

Once I reached the desired size, he would put just a tad more saline in to allow wiggle room during the switch out surgery. I would hold at that size for six to eight weeks, and then they would do the switcheroo: replacing the expanders with silicone implants.

Unfortunately, I was terrified of surgery itself and of dying on the table. I told Dr. Pearl to have the paddles ready just in case; hell, I was telling everybody to have them within an arm's reach. I explained that my grandfather hemorrhaged and died in his thirties following a surgery, and my mom hemorrhaged and flat lined (she survived) following a surgery in her twenties. Needless to say, I was petrified of a similar fate. I had no idea if this was genetic or bad luck, but I wasn't taking any chances. The cancer had to go, so I desperately needed surgery. Dr. Pearl was kind and compassionate. He also told me not to worry, that I would *not* die on the table. Our biggest risk, he said, would be infection.

He confirmed with me that I would be doing a bilateral mastectomy. This would make life easier for me for two reasons. One, I wouldn't have to live my life with a time bomb ticking on my left breast; and two, if I did them at the same time, he would make sure that my boobs matched—that I had symmetry. *Yep, sign me up. Take them both because I sure as hell am not going through this again.*

Token of Courage: Keep an Open Mind

More than anything, this experience reiterated to me the importance of having an open mind. Walking through life with horse blinders on only dims your true understanding of the world. Learning to toss those blinders to the wayside opens up a whole new world of vision. This holds merit for all of us!

In life, things are not always what they seem; people are not always who you have made them out to be. You don't truly know about something or someone unless you take the time to find out for yourself. Don't understand another's religion? Ask them about it. Someone acts differently than you? Comes from a different culture? Has different perspectives or priorities? Hear them out. Put down your judgement, peel those blinders off, and keep an open mind. You may not necessarily agree, but the world will grow—and so will you—when you gain depth perception; and in turn, compassion will flourish and both you and the world will be changed for the better.

We are all guilty of being judgmental at times. We think something or someone is *all* good or *all* bad, but the truth is we are made up of both. Turns out, when we bench our biases long enough to hear about something different and keep an open mind, we grow in our courage. My adjusted vision saw plastic surgery for what it *really* was. It was a life raft for me, and the life vest on board was sewn with hope. Furthermore, the idea of losing both breasts instead of the tainted one alone was a HUGE adjustment. It was hard enough to say goodbye to part of me; but with an open mind, I found courage to say goodbye to both. It was the best choice for me, and I have no regrets.

Chapter 6

Mommy Has a Booboo

Nugget of Knowledge

In one of my 2019 *Keepers of the Flame*® podcast interviews, Jen Davis described what it meant to be at an elevated risk for acquiring breast cancer. Jen explained that the Tyrer-Cuzick model was a software program for predicting overall lifetime risk of getting breast cancer for individuals. It took into account the patient's family history, hereditary mutations, personal risk factors, age, height, weight, age at first delivery, Ashkenazi Jewish descent, hormone use, breast density, among other factors, and then generated a score (Williams 2019, Episode 28).

If the Tyrer-Cuzick score is less than 15%, then a woman is at average risk. Intermediate risk would be if the score is between 15% and 19%, whereas anything over 20% lifetime-risk is deemed high risk. High risk patients are often recommended for annual mammograms and MRIs alternating every six months (Williams, 2019, Episode 28).

Hereditary cancer mutations, such as the BRCA mutations, can elevate a lifetime risk of getting breast cancer to well over 80%, sometimes even up to a 90% chance, depending on other risk factors. Hereditary mutations can increase one's risk for other cancers as well. For example, I have the BRCA2 mutation, thus a high risk of getting breast cancer (84% lifetime risk for me), ovarian cancer, and pancreatic cancer, along with an elevated risk for melanoma.

Personal Voyage

Because the BRCA2 mutation also increased my likelihood of getting ovarian cancer, I knew that doctors would want to take my ovaries next as a prophylactic measurement against my risk for ovarian cancer; and frankly, part of me wanted them out too. Get the safe havens for cancer cells the fuck out of my body, and let me live my life. Evict the terrorist cells and squash their prospective camps. I was, after all, planning to live to 95. Yet, that surgery would have to wait until after the completion of my mastectomy.

Even though there was not a reliable screening method for ovarian cancer, part of my aggressive surveillance strategy with my OBGYN included yearly ultrasounds of my ovaries. My OB was well aware of the drama unfolding with my breasts, and when I asked if this ultrasound could wait until school started up in August, he told me no. I think he was being protective and thorough, wanting to be sure that nothing resembling cancer was in my ovaries.

Thankfully, all looked well with my ovaries. Phew! At least one bullet was dodged for the time being. As I was leaving, I spoke with the nurse, who I adored; she was always so supportive of me, and she spoke to me as a friend and said that if a double mastectomy was what I wanted, not to let *anyone* deter me. She shared that a friend of hers was pressured into NOT doing the double, only to have the 'good' breast taken later; and then another friend had argued for doctors to take both, only to discover after a biopsy that there was indeed cancer growing in the 'good' breast too.

While I waited for both surgeons to coordinate their schedules and give me a surgery date, I had to prepare both logistically and emotionally. Logistics were a bit easier to tame than the complexity of my emotions. Those damn things were unruly; still, I stuffed them away as much as I could. I was not yet in a place where I was willing to tend to emotions; I was action driven. I was living in fight or flight survival mode. I was afraid the emotions would bring me down, and in my mind, I couldn't afford to be weak. I wanted to win, and I wrongfully equated these swirling negative emotions with weakness. I didn't yet understand that they are part of the uniquely woven threads of our humanity.

I had been a handful of times to see my therapist, Ashley, but it was still not something I had made public just yet. The only people who knew were my husband and my best friend. At this point, I was still heavily guarded, perhaps even a bit ashamed that I couldn't seem to handle my own troubles. Still, I took comfort in knowing I had a place to go and get unbiased, professional advice and support. I needed that in these dreary days more than ever, despite feeling like I had to hide it from the world.

My mom, one of my all-time forever heroes, said she would be there whenever Bryan and I needed her. It was a huge relief to know that our kids would be well cared for, both during and after surgery. I would be physically out of the game, and Bryan would need to tend to me. I also began to plan for how to protect and support my kids and their emotions.

I was incredibly anxious about telling my kids that I had cancer and needed surgery. I didn't want to lie or hide things from them, but they needed a kid-friendly, G-rated version of what was happening to Mommy. I wanted to protect them while still being honest, and I didn't want any part of my story to elicit fear in their minds: fear for Mommy or fear of their own bodies. I pressured myself to say things *just right*. My girls were my whole world, and I didn't want to shatter any sense of security for them. I wanted to buffer their potential worry and fear, absorb them myself if I had to, and protect the sacredness of their childhood. Still, it was critical they were told *something*. They needed the truth without the gory details.

Ashley and I discussed strategies of how to tell my kids—then four and five years old—the news, and together we came up with a plan. *I could do this.* One evening, as we were preparing for bedtime, I had Sage and Leona sit together on the bed, took a deep breath, and with my calmest Mommy-voice, I launched in:

"Girls, I need to tell you something important."

They both sat there with big eyes and got unusually quiet.

"Mommy has a booboo. The booboo I have is in my breast," I said, pointing to the site of the "booboo."

Their eyes followed my hand to my breast and then back to my eyes.

"The kind of booboo Mommy has can't be fixed with Neosporin and a Band-Aid. I need to go to the hospital where doctors have special cameras and tools to be able to take the booboo away; and since I have to go to the hospital, Grandma will be coming to visit and stay with you."

They erupted with excitement.

"Hooray!!! Grandma's coming!" Leona jumped up and down with her upper body alone, and Sage clapped her little hands together with joy.

"This is gonna be the best summer *ever!*" Leona screamed.

I smiled and relaxed as I was reminded of their sweet

innocence; I took comfort in that. "Yes! I know, you love Grandma!" I waited until they calmed down and then continued, "Now, just like your friend needed to rest after she had her tonsils removed, Mommy will be tired and need some rest when I come home from the hospital."

They seemed to understand and were still very excited about Grandma's pending visit.

"Okay, so, if you have any questions about this, I want you to know you can ask me and I'll do my very best to answer them."

Leona, my little five-year-old problem solver, asked the first one: "Mommy, how do they get the booboo out?"

My heart pounded, but I continued, as strong as I could be: "Well, the doctors went to school to learn lots of different ways to take care of different booboos; each booboo has a different procedure, and they know which one to use for mine." I was proud of Leona for her insight and questions, and my answer seemed to be enough for the time being.

Sage, my precious four-year-old, looked up after hearing my answer and, with eyes as wide as quarters, said: "Mommy, the only thing that I know how to cure is hiccups!"

With this, my anxiety peeled away, I smiled and gave them both gigantic hugs, burying my face between their little-girl-sweetness. "I love you two SO MUCH!"

They giggled and hugged me back even tighter.

*   *   *

Life continued, and I insisted on shielding my loved ones from my internal pain. I wanted to protect them. I would later come

Fig. 3. Leona before her sixth birthday party at the roller-skating rink

to realize the power in vulnerability, but for the time being, I wanted none of that.

Leona was turning six and wanted a birthday party at the roller-skating rink. So, I mustered up some form of strength, summoned my internal planner, and made it happen. I think Leona skated for the entire two hours we were there; she laughed, grinned from ear to ear, and never once slowed down. It warmed my heart to see such happiness in my children. I was glad to be able to give her that day. I leaned against the skating rink wall and paused for a moment as I watched friends—both Leona's and mine—skating and smiling.

For a moment my face turned sad as I thought about how this disease growing inside of me had the potential to rip this happiness away. I shuttered at the thought of these evil cells plaguing my breast. I wanted them gone. I wanted to reclaim my body, and I wanted it now! After recognizing this wasn't something that I could control, I shook the thought away and smiled at my birthday girl as she shouted for me to watch her once more.

Life continued in other ways as well. There were playdates and birthday parties, followed by prepping for the start of school. I knew my abilities would be hindered after surgery, so I wanted to prepare in advance.

Depending on when surgery was in July, it was possible I wouldn't be well enough to make it to the school's open house. This crushed my spirit just a little bit—okay, it stomped on it and ripped it to shreds. I know it's silly, but it made me feel like a rotten mom. I wanted to be there for my girls; I wanted to celebrate *all* the moments of their lives. I wanted to be *Mom*; and I was pissed that cancer was getting in my way.

Bryan was processing things at his own pace and in his own way. Initially, I would get annoyed by his research mode; I thought he was trying to poke holes in my plan. However, he was merely processing this blow in his own way; he was trying to gather as much information about my cancer and its treatment and prognosis in an effort to piece things together, perhaps to feel like we had some control. He was heartbroken that this was happening to *his* wife. He desperately wanted to wake from this nightmare. He loved me and wanted to protect me and keep me safe.

Bryan did two rather remarkable things for me before my surgery. One of the most amazing things he did for me was to share a YouTube video he found. It was ironic that part of his internet digging I despised brought about something so wonderful. The video was of a breast cancer survivor who spoke of the top five reasons why she loved her mastectomy. The girl was crazy! I liked her immediately. She was bold, fearless, and found humor and fun in a rotten situation. Plus, her fake boobs didn't look half bad. She even showed how her implants could glow in the dark (McGuinness 2015). *Say what? I was going to have glow-in-the-dark boobs?* I laughed so hard and smiled so big that my cheeks hurt. I hadn't laughed like that in weeks! True or not, *that* was an experiment I wanted to test!

The second thing that Bryan did for me was a surprise— he coordinated and hired a photographer to take *Goddess Sessions* of me. He wanted me to feel beautiful, to know from the inside who I *really* was. He wanted me to do a *Before the Storm, During the Storm,* and *On the Other Side* photo shoot. It was one of the most beautiful and empowering experiences of my life. I was able to connect with the world around me and harvest from within myself my own true beauty: my courage, strength, vulnerability, and resolve. I felt these true colors shine through both my laughter and my tears. I felt what it meant to be beautiful, to be real, to be me; and to own all of that throughout the journey, despite my trepidation along the way. This was me: the complete vulnerable, scared, determined, fearful, smiley self. I began to take ownership of every bit of my body, mind, and soul.

Fig. 4, Photo of Joyce 'Before the Storm', summer of 2017
Photograph by Mackensey Alexander

Fig. 5, Photo of Joyce 'Before the Storm'
Photograph by Mackensey Alexander

I soon received notification of my surgery date. July 17, 2017 would be the day I would lose my breasts. This was not going to be easy. I was scared of the surgery, of not waking up, of the cancer spreading, of unwrapping my bandages and hating what I saw in the mirror. I cried, and I prayed, and I reminded myself of the Ambrose Redmoon (1991) quote: "Courage is not the absence of fear, but rather the judgement that something else is more important than one's fear… To take action regardless of fear is brave."

I had an overwhelming desire to make good come from this rotten hand I'd been dealt. It seemed like a necessity; there was a strong call, a pull in that direction. I decided I wanted to write, to document the entire journey. I didn't want to gloss over or downplay the middle. I wanted to write it all, to show *how* I made it to the other side.

I also wanted to show my girls that when you're knocked down and don't feel like you have the strength to get back up, if you keep moving through the tunnel, you'll get there. Baby steps are still steps.

Token of Courage: To Fear Is Human

I did a quick Google search on the word *courage,* and it came up that courage was "strength in the face of pain or grief." Synonyms for the word included *fearlessness.* I think this is misleading. In my opinion, Ambrose Redmoon is the one who nailed the definition. Although fear had become my unwanted traveling companion, *courage* did not criticize me for it.

I crept forward with my survival plan and continued to live my life despite the terror of an early death. I had the courage to face a double mastectomy to treat my cancer, courage to consider a prophylactic hysterectomy to account for my mutation and elevated risk, courage to have a tough conversation with my children, and courage to ground myself and accept that I would soon be drastically changed. I had courage to live life, to plan birthday parties and playdates, all during this unpredictable and unsettling time. However, make no mistake about it: There was fear! I was petrified!

Acquiring the sixth courage token requires you to separate those two words: courage and fearlessness. You can be courageous and still be afraid. Having courage means that you move forward with what you know in your gut needs to be done, despite the fear riding shotgun. To be afraid is to be human.

Chapter 7

The Cost of Living

Nugget of Knowledge

Remember my therapist's advice about letting go of what you can't control and focusing on what you can? Well, preparing for surgery, physically and emotionally, is something you *can* do.

Physically, once you've gathered your data and decided on a treatment plan, then it's time to prepare for things you'll need before and after surgery. If you have a mastectomy, you'll need to arrange for someone to take over the reins for approximately two weeks. Cooking, laundry, driving—dish those responsibilities out for others to take care of you. You will need to rest, and you won't be able to move your arms or torso as easily as you could prior to surgery.

Get some soft skirts and button-up tops. Following a mastectomy, your range of motion is significantly impacted, and putting clothes on over your head just isn't possible. It gets better with time, but following surgery it will be hard to move. Button-up tops are therefore a must-have. I also liked long, soft skirts as opposed to any sort of pants because the pants required much more pulling and tugging to get on and off. With skirts, you can simply put your hands by your side and use your fingers to crinkle up the skirt so that you can sit on the toilet, do your thing, stand, and then drop the skirt.

While I had the drains, I wasn't permitted to shower either. So, arm yourself with bath wipes, dry shampoo, and perhaps even an electric razor. An electric toothbrush can also provide some relief. The back-and-forth motion of brushing teeth can be excruciating, whereas an electric toothbrush can do the work for you.

You'll want a small pillow to accompany you in the car on the way home from the hospital; it will protect your wounds from the seatbelt. Also, you'll want to have a place set up for you to sleep when you get home. Some people use recliners; I used my couch with lots and lots of pillows.

When people want to help you, let them! Meal trains are a great way for your family and friends to show up for you. Having someone clean your house is a lifesaver too, because you won't be able to move or lift in that way. A "ponytail fund" was perhaps one of my favorite things. Since I wasn't able to manage my own hair after surgery, my aunt set me up with the ability to go to the salon every few days to have my stylist wash and dry my hair for me. It was amazing how much more human I felt with a clean head of hair.

If you don't remember any of my advice, remember this for the day of surgery: You will be conscious when they roll you into the surgical room, and your brain may try to look around in efforts to process what's happening. *Don't.* Instead, focus on one nurse. Make it your brain's mission to remember anything and everything about that one nurse. Make it your job to be able to write a biography about her, and then your brain will let the rest of the room drown out in the background. I didn't know to do this for my first surgery, and it later became a source of some PTSD symptoms. However, I did it for my second surgery, and I don't remember any of it.

Personal Voyage

Leona woke me in the early hours of the morning the day of my surgery; she had a nightmare. She stood at the edge of my bed, and her eyes filled with tears, as she said through sobs, "Mommy, I had a bad dream." Normally I'd give her a big hug, hold her for a few minutes, talk about it, explain that she was safe, that her dream couldn't hurt her, and then walk her back to her room and tuck her in with more kisses.

On this early morning, however, I did all but walk her back to her room. Instead, I let my little girl climb into bed next to me and snuggle as long as she wanted. She stayed next to me until the alarm called for me to rise, and while she clung to me, I was reminded of all that I held dear and exactly why I was doing what I was doing that day. I let her stay because I knew that after the surgery it would be awhile before I could hold her close again. I wanted to savor this snuggle; I wanted to be there for her, both now (in the aftermath of a bad dream) and in all the tomorrows we had left to dream up. I would enjoy these cuddles, and then wake up and fight like hell for my family, for my life.

Grandma was there to take care of the girls while Bryan took me to the hospital. Her plan was to stay until I recovered enough to be able to function, drive, and be more or less back on my feet (which turned out to be about three weeks). Bryan and I kissed Leona and Sage goodbye, said our farewells, and headed off towards Savannah.

It seemed appropriate that while in route giant raindrops began to plop on our windshield. Soon, they began racing from the sky so fast they united into a sheet of water that pounded our car and attempted to obscure our view. It was a match between water and wipers, and the water seemed to have the upper hand. Flashes of light soon lit up the darkness followed by booming rolls of thunder. The frequency of sound and light increased, and thunder did its best to keep up with lightning. I snickered a little when I realized that my metaphor was becoming my reality: I was quite literally driving into the storm!

We arrived at the hospital safely, parked in the garage, and even managed to make it to the hospital door as we escaped through a tiny reprieve in the storm. As soon as we entered the building, however, the curtains of the storm fell once again. Was this not an unsettling start to the day?

We checked in and while signing a few forms, Bryan joked with the attendant, "We'd like the penthouse, please!"

A smile grew upon the man's face as he chuckled out loud and shook his head, "Oh boy! Nah man, you don't want the penthouse here."

"What? Why? Wait, is that the morgue?"

I chimed in, joking about renegotiating our request, "No! No, we definitely don't want the penthouse. You can keep it. We're good."

The three of our cheeks were flushed, red with embarrassment and laughter. He told us that it was actually their ICU. All the same, we didn't want that either.

Soon, they called me back. They had Bryan wait in the waiting room first. They wanted to get me back, changed, and all hooked up prior to having a guest. So, I went by myself to face the gown, the socks, and the uncertainty of what was to come. I removed all of my clothes, put on the patient gown (the one that screams I'm in the hospital, I'm sick, my robe won't close), and then fought to put on the compression hose. They looked like panty hose, but I assure you, they were not. Their goal was to eliminate the potential for blood clots during surgery, however those sons-a-bitches did not want to go on my calves. On top of them, I was to wear these red socks with grips on all sides. I climbed into the gurney, clicked my ruby-red-slippered heels together, and thought to myself how nice it would be if only that would take me home and make this nightmare go away. I wasn't in OZ though, and it didn't work.

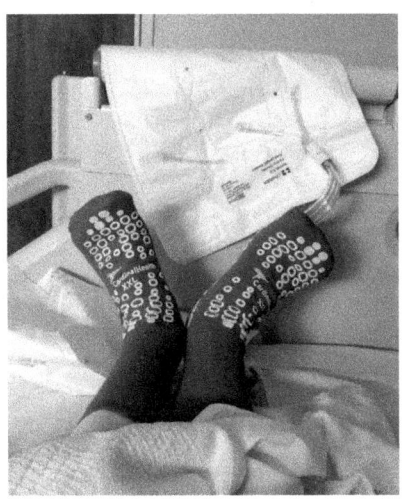

Fig. 6. Joyce's red surgery socks during bilateral mastectomy. July 2017.

Dr. Rehl made her rounds and checked on me. She answered a few questions about the surgery and reassured me that this was "treatable and curable." I, of course, reminded her about my family's hemorrhaging history. I was a bit apprehensive about the operating room, but I appreciated that Dr. Rehl was personable, calm, and encouraging. She also told me that she would do a preliminary check of the nodes during surgery, but they wouldn't have the full results until about a week later. She gave a warm smile, offered a "see you soon," and left.

I was relatively calm; I kind of surprised myself. I wanted the cancer out! Cut it out! Make it go away! I was doing my best to stay optimistic and find the humor where I could. I was scared of the surgery, but I was more scared of letting the cancer go unchecked.

Bryan soon joined me in this holding tank of a room. Nuclear medicine dropped by to inject their tracer into my breast. Damn did that hurt! They stuck the needle in close proximity to my nipple, which was not only a sensitive place, but the needle was sharp and it stung. This radiotracer was what they used to help locate the nodes that needed to be removed; so, I endured and survived.

Soon, a nurse came and gave me a delightful cocktail of "I-don't-give-a-shit" medicine. It was fantastic and lived up to the fake name that I gave it because *I did not give a shit*. I was relaxed and spacey. My dearest husband took videos of me and all my loopiness to share with family and friends.

My surgery time was quickly approaching; I kissed Bryan goodbye, and they wheeled me down the hall and around a few corners. Everything looked very "hospitalesque." Nurses were in scrubs. There were other folks in white coats and masks; and there was hospital equipment and gurneys throughout the halls. It felt very surreal. I was being rolled through this hall. It wasn't a movie or a sitcom. It was real life; it was *my* life, and I wasn't entirely sure how much longer it was going to last.

They rolled me into the operating room, which was even more intimidating. Everything was so sterile, which of course is a good thing; but it also reinforced the reality and magnitude of what was happening to me. I was scared, nervous, and my "I-don't-give-a-shit" cocktail was failing me. Terror began to roll through my body, and an intense overwhelming panic soon accompanied my loopiness.

I had to climb out of my gurney and onto a table…THE table. It was the table where they would be taking knives to my flesh and ripping it off of me. There were giant lights that hung over me, and I could see nurses on the side of the room counting (*and I imagined sharpening*) shiny silver flesh piercing tools. It looked like a torture chamber, a horror film; and yet this was real life.

Nurses who were tending to me tried to explain what they were doing over there. Still, I'm sure my vitals didn't express any relief, so they tried to distract me with questions about my family. I was shaking, panicking. Dr. Rehl was over to my left prepping for surgery, and she smiled at me and calmly said my name, "Hi Joyce." The anxiety I felt may have paused slightly with her reassuring smile, but as my head shifted again to the right, and I saw the knives, my overwhelming inescapable fear did not dissipate; it grew more intense.

They continued to prep me by strapping my body down. I remember the belt getting tightened across my legs. I was getting tied down, trapped, pinned inside this horrifying torture room. I felt tears well up in my eyes. *What was happening to me?*

A man I recognized from earlier appeared next to me; he was the anesthesiologist, and my eyes begged him to save me. *Please rescue me. Please, give me drugs! Help me escape from here!* He soon placed a mask over my face, but then I realized what was about to happen the moment that I lost consciousness. *Those shiny silver knives in the corner would soon puncture my flesh and carve off part of my body.* With an ache in my heart and tremors in my soul, fear pumped through my veins. His green scrubs and beard were the last things that I saw as my vision disappeared, and I drifted away.

I have a few fuzzy memories of when I first woke up. I opened my eyes and heard mumbles of people talking. Soon I could recognize that they were nurses. Patients were lined up in a row on gurneys in this dimly lit room; and the two nurses were tending to each of us, monitoring our conditions post-surgeries, and hooking up morphine drips. While I waited my turn, I remembered where I was and what I had just survived; I was alive. I didn't die!

I was groggy but grateful, and then I remembered what my surgery had taken from me. I glanced under my gown to see what was left of me. However, they had me bandaged up pretty well and all that I saw was a white surgical bra. My imagination was all that could describe what existed underneath, but I was too tired to think.

My surgery had started at noon, the mastectomy was over at 3:10 p.m., and the second surgery was over at 5:49 p.m. Bryan had been waiting for a long time. After my morphine drip was hooked up and Bryan was by my side, they wheeled me into my overnight room around 8:00 p.m. It had been a long day!

Nurses came every so often to check on me and empty my drains. There were two drains on each side of me that hung on Velcro loops of a special belt. The grenade-like plastic drains were attached to my body with a tube, and the tube was held into place with a single stitch or two. The tubes (each about the diameter of a straw) disappeared into my body and traveled to cavities around the expanders where my breasts once were. The drains would fill with liquid from within: blood coupled with God-only-knew-what. Somehow the tubes put pressure in places that made it difficult to breathe. I

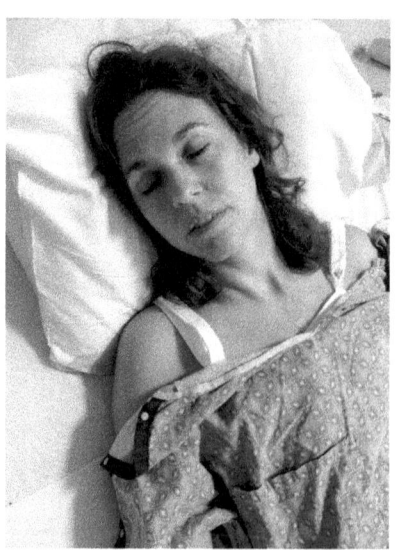

Fig. 7. Joyce in the hospital post mastectomy surgery in July 2017

wanted to take shallow breaths to ease any discomfort; however, I was given a tool to practice deep breathing. These exercises were essential to clear my lungs and prevent the development of pneumonia.

Every now and then I would rise to use the restroom and tote my drip alongside me. Getting back into bed was incredibly difficult and tiring. My chest muscles had been ripped and stretched, my breasts were gone, and the use of my arms was just not possible. I could not use my arms to lift myself up or to scooch over on the bed. I sat on the edge of the bed and a nurse tried to help me by lifting and rotating my legs for me. *Holy shit did that hurt!* It contorted my torso in such a way that pulled on my nonexistent muscle strength in my chest and tugged on my freshly sown wounds. This was going to take some getting used to. After every trip to the restroom and the exhausting, painful attempt to reposition myself back into bed, I needed morphine.

Eventually, my drip was done, and they gave me oral pain meds instead. I tried to use them sparingly but to also not be stupid and deny them altogether. The pain was still very fresh. Walking was supposed to be good for you, and I was motivated to heal quickly and regain my life. So, Bryan took me on a walk. Baby steps were all that I could muster as we shuffled down the length of the hallway. I held his arm but couldn't rely on it for more than balance. I couldn't use my arms or my chest muscles for guidance. My strength and mobility had to come from my legs and my core alone. That was all that I could count on to move, to sit up, and to do anything.

Another man was escorting his wife on a walk post-surgery as well. The two of us women smiled at each other through our mutual understanding of one another's agony. Her husband joked with us, "Hey, want to race?" I thought it was hysterical as I could only imagine what a sight the two of us were as we hobbled in pain through the hall post-surgery. I started to chuckle at the thought, but laughing hurt my stitches immensely, so I settled for a smile.

Doctors came to see how I was doing as well. Dr. Rehl was a phenomenal surgeon, and I liked and trusted her a great deal. My OBGYN had been at the hospital and knew of my surgery, so he stopped by to check on me. My face lit up when I saw him. I was appreciative of his concern and thankful for him and his diligence. He was one of the reasons I found my cancer early. He was there with me through the genetic testing, through ordering mammograms and MRIs, and through this cancer phase as well. Even back when I got my initial biopsy results, although he knew I'd been notified, he still called to check on me.

Token of Courage: Look Up!

When I ran high school cross country half a million years ago, our coaches would often tell us two things, and this coaching advice proved especially beneficial when our bodies became fatigued.

First, they told us to use our arms. Now, I know it sounds silly to say "use your arms" in order to run, but it works. It works because when you focus your attention on your form, pull your arms up to 90-degree angles, and move them parallel to your body—when you make these fine tune adjustments—somehow you hurt less, feel stronger and more in control, and the rest of your stride and body alignment adjust appropriately.

So, when you are becoming fatigued in your own life, try focusing on fine tuning an aspect of your life that you can actually control. Make those minor adjustments and watch how they can impact the rest of your body and mind. It's shifting that perspective!

The second thing my coaches would tell us to do is quite simple. "Look up! Keep your eyes on the horizon!" Don't stare at the dirt right in front of your feet; rather, look up and watch where you are going! Watch the trees in the distance getting closer to you with *every* single step, and when you pass that tree, keep your eyes up and focus on the next. Keep making those incremental goals. Keep those eyes lifted and soon you'll see the flags at the end of your hardship.

Along the way, my *trees*, *houses*, and *fencepost* goals were: taking my kids to school, showering, getting my own damn food from the fridge, having my hair washed, going school shopping.

Take my coaches' advice: when the going gets tough, don't look down—look up!

Chapter 8

The Charm and T-Rex Arms

Nugget of Knowledge

Immediately post-surgery, I was groggy, in pain, and slow to move. Sitting on my own was excruciatingly painful; getting up to go to the bathroom required *all* of my energy and warranted naps. Recovery was slow-going. But we cannot run until we walk; we cannot walk until we crawl. It is hard to learn this all over again as an adult; but rising up from a fall doesn't always happen overnight.

Two University of Melbourne researchers (Leslie and Allen 2017) explain why you may feel exhausted and unable to do things without fatigue immediately following an operation. First, they explain that "general anesthesia is a reversible drug-induced coma" that prevents the patient from feeling pain or remembering anything—a necessity for painful and traumatic procedures. However, with that comes some side-effects. The effects of anesthesia may linger for a few days. Additionally, Leslie and Allen explain: "The surgery itself causes tissue injury. After surgery, your body undergoes repair and recovery, which drives a higher baseline metabolic rate and draws on your nutrient stores. So, it isn't surprising that such intense activity at a cellular level results in feeling tired after surgery."

All of this coupled with the physical limitations of the mastectomy itself are cause for fatigue. Your body is having to repair not only from the outside, but also on a cellular/tissue level internally. This will take energy and time.

Healing from physical and emotional wounds takes time and support from others. We can't expect ourselves to jump up immediately following a crash and operate at full steam. It takes time to heal, so try not to compare yourself to who you were prior to your fall, and focus more instead on the small victories you achieve after your face plant. These tiny triumphs will add up over time.

Knowing this, accepting this, and still choosing to inch forward however slowly it feels, will be your ticket to healing.

Personal Voyage

After two nights in the hospital, I was finally released and allowed to finish my recovery at home. I was still on pain meds, so my memories are a little "druggy." I remember them wheeling me out of the building and Bryan going to get the car to pick me up from the loop right outside. The use of my arms was still not possible, so I couldn't use them to push myself up from the wheelchair. Instead, I used my core and my legs to shuffle myself to the edge of the seat and then gently rise with my quads. I took incredibly slow, small steps to the passenger side door. Once I was in the car, I needed help buckling in. I felt a little helpless, although my disdain for not being self-sufficient didn't rise just yet. It was kept at bay with the aloofness accompanying my pain meds; I was helpless, but I didn't give a rat's ass—at least not then.

When we arrived at the house, my mom had taken the girls to the neighborhood pool. She wanted me to have a chance to get home and settle in with some quiet, maybe even take a nap. *Moms are smart!*

I knew there was no way that I'd be able to sleep in my bed. It was a normal height king bed, but it was still too high for me to get into without the use of my torso. I struggled enough with getting into bed at the hospital. So, I knew that I'd be setting up camp on the couch. When I rounded the corner to the living room, I saw that Mom and the girls had "made" my new bed. The couch was covered with Wonder Woman sheets, turned down with a soft blanket, and set to go with tons of fluffy pillows. *You rock, Mom!* I did my version of "climbing in" and then crashed. The trip home had worn me out.

Fig. 8. Joyce, Leona, and Sage with Kindness Rocks recovering at home in July 2017

Soon Mom, Leona, and Sage came back, and the girls ran right up to me. They were so excited to see me. They had to give me "fairy kisses" and "hand hugs" instead of normal hugs and kisses. It was hard for me, but I think that they liked that this was somehow different and special.

They became my best cheerleaders for my breathing exercises. Every time Sage passed me, she would hand me my breathing tool and say, "Here Mom. It's time to exercise." Then she and Leona would cheer as loudly as they could for me to make my mark on the tool. "Go, Mommy, go!" they shouted. I was proud of them. They also made me pictures to decorate my new room, and we hung them from the mantle so I could see them every day.

Almost as soon as I returned home, the dryer broke. All I remember about this was my mom and Bryan asking me if I had any input on buying a dryer. My only response was, *"Blue."* I had no idea what I was talking about or where I came up with blue, but at least I wasn't in charge. I fell back asleep and let the other adults figure out my dryer situation.

Later that same day, Sage lost a tooth. It was a damn good thing that the Tooth Fairy in our house was always prepared. I may have been sick and loopy, but the Tooth Fairy had to come regardless. I managed to find the stash of fairy prizes and passed the torch to Grandma. I crashed again.

There was an outpouring of support from my family and friends. Michelle had orchestrated a meal train and had people bringing us food every Monday, Wednesday, and Friday. Friends both locally and across the country brought or sent food, flowers, gifts, and notes with kind words. I felt blessed to have such loving people in my corner. The support and prayers I received were endless and so appreciated.

My Kappa Kappa Gamma sorority sisters got me a lighthouse charm to remind me that there was always light in the darkness. I wore it every day on a bracelet to remind myself I was going to be okay, that I would make it through this rough patch. It was this beautiful symbol of hope that guided and comforted me through my darkest seas. The lighthouse would soon become the symbol for the non-profit I founded: Keepers of the Flame® Foundation. The name, Keepers of the Flame, fit right along with lighthouse imagery since lighthouses were once lit with real flames. It was as if all the women who had walked this road before me helped brighten the light and softly whispered, "You're not alone." They were my keepers of the flame…and together, they lit the path with their stories, their tears, and their triumphs.

That little lighthouse gave me hope when I saw myself without bandages for the first time in the bathroom mirror just days after my surgery. My scars were fresh, and I couldn't help but burst into tears. My body looked like a war zone. The stitches were there, covered with dried blood and medical glue. My breasts were gone. They were *gone*!

My chest looked like a man's that had been mauled. I had more stitches under my right arm from where they removed lymph nodes. I studied the four tubes that hung from me. Where the drains entered my body, they each entered through a hole. A *hole* on the surface of my flesh! I had *four* holes! You could see the tubes sliding into my body and then blood hung in the grenade-like drains. I no longer saw myself. *Who was this stranger staring at me in the mirror?*

Then, I caught a glance of my lighthouse hanging on my wrist, and it reminded me of all the brave women who had come before me. It allowed me to muster up enough courage and resolve to keep creeping forward. Ever so slowly, I kept breathing, inching my way through recovery. It was heartbreaking, but the alternative—giving up and dying—was not an option. I was determined to be there for my husband and our girls; I just had to make it through this rocky patch.

After about a week, I was completely off of all pain meds. My mind cleared up, and I could focus and think again. I was relieved to have my mind back. I was glad to be rid of the medicine. My body didn't get this memo, and it was not recovering quite as swiftly. This only fueled frustration and disappointment within me. I could hear my daughters' sweet voices and goofy laughs as they played in the other room. Heartbreak ensued as I couldn't will my body to do more. I tried to remind myself that what I was going through was a requirement for not missing out on future moments. Still, my heart stung and I missed my babies.

I tried to venture out of the house a few times. I went to Walmart to try and pick up a few more school supplies. I thought I was hot stuff for going shopping. Unfortunately, walking the length of the aisles wore me out. I felt sick and weak, and I had to sit down. I was frustrated again with my body's inability to do as I wanted. I hated that I got tired, that I couldn't do simple things. It was Walmart, for goodness sake! Still, the length of the aisles had somehow grown since I was there last, or so it seemed.

One afternoon, I woke from a nap and wanted to get some lunch from the refrigerator. I was determined to do it for myself, so I staggered to the kitchen. It took all of my strength to open the left side of the refrigerator door. Dang it! What I wanted was on the right side. I laughed at myself a bit, and then I muscled up and tried to open the other side. Success! I got it open. I stood in the kitchen, with both doors to the fridge ajar, and stared in disbelief at the food that I wanted. It was on the top fucking shelf! I couldn't reach that! My little t-rex arms would not stretch to such lengths. About that time, Mom walked in and rescued me from my predicament. I laughed in spite of myself.

I had the drains for the first two weeks post-surgery; and while sporting those undesired accessories, I was unable to take a real shower. I had to take a sponge bath while standing in the bathroom. At first, I tried using cleansing wipes, but I despised the smell. I *hated* being the stinky kid; I wanted real, honest-to-

God soap! So, I armed myself with my own body wash, a wash cloth, towels, and the bathroom sink.

I also wanted to shave, but reaching under my arms was quite the struggle. Not only could I not raise my arms very high after having my chest cut off, but I also had stitches underneath my right arm that had to be dodged. I tried everything. Straight razors were a bad idea. I had also lost some sensation under my arm and couldn't tell how hard I was pushing against my skin. I had no idea whether or not I was on the verge of slicing skin or popping a stitch. I finally had the best of luck using an electric razor. Even so, I wasn't able to get a clean shave and that bugged me. Even with sponge baths, make-shift shaving, and deodorant, I still felt stinky, which made me want to cry. Cancer had stolen my breasts AND my ability for daily hygiene. I knew this was temporary, but it was still difficult to see past the present pain.

Before I could leave the bathroom, I still needed to get dressed and drain the drains. Bryan helped me with those. The whole process of getting dressed and ready for the day took me over an hour—and that didn't include my hair. I was exhausted and in pain by the end of it, and I needed a nap. *How discouraging!*

Getting dressed and ready for the day are rituals that most of us do with little thought. We take our ability to move, to shower, and to take care of basic hygiene for granted. I was looking forward to having my drains removed. Not only were those things gross, but I *really* wanted to take a shower. I wanted my autonomy back; and I wanted the stink gone.

I went to see Dr. Pearl to remove the drains. Nurses removed the first two drains about a week after surgery, and they removed the last two drains by the end of the second week. Both times were excruciatingly painful. They cut the stitch that held the tube to my side and then told me to take a deep breath. As I inhaled, the nurse yanked the tube out of my body. Skin and tissue from within must have started to cling to the tubes internally because I felt as if my insides were getting yanked out as well. I screamed and then the tube was out. After the initial shock and trauma, I cried.

The nurse was so kind. She rubbed my shoulder, got me a tissue, and gave me a minute before moving to the other side. However, when she went to the other side to remove the next drain and asked me to inhale, I said, "No. I don't want to breathe." I was a quick learner and knew that breathing led to pain. I didn't want to do that again. I did want those drains gone, though, and there was only one way to make that happen: be tough. So, I eventually complied and took another deep breath and endured more pain.

Blood and bits of tissue rested on the towel in front of me as Bryan and I studied them closely. I endured this torture *four* times. There were *four* drains, so there were *four* tubes to remove. However, the relief that accompanied this unpleasantness was immense and worth every bit of agony. I could finally take deep breaths with ease, I felt more mobile and more human-like, and I was given permission to take a real shower!

I was looking forward to feeling the water run down my body, for soap to get a good lather, and to rinse the stink I had acquired. I was pleased with myself and stepped into the shower, yet before the water even touched what was left of my breasts, I had intense pain on my right set of stitches. It felt like something from within was trying to pry the stitches open. It moved across the stitches from the inside, pushing outward against them as it moved. I screamed in agony and Bryan came running. I didn't know what to do. I became frightened of the water, of placing myself in the stream as if that somehow triggered the internal pain.

Slowly, I regained some courage and began to inch my way back into the stream once more. This was not easy or relaxing. I couldn't reach any of my shampoo or body wash; Bryan had to place them on the floor so that I could get to them. Bending down only intimidated me at the prospects of triggering more movement beneath my stitches. I managed to finish bathing and then dried off; all the while, tears raced down my cheeks. *What was happening to me?*

Bryan and I looked at my right side where I felt that movement and pain, and we noticed that a knot of some kind had moved closer to my armpit. A bruise started to form there. We called the doctor, and he told us that it sounded like a flap of the expander had unfolded. There was nothing for us to worry about; it was okay.

My first shower experience post-surgery was needless to say a bit rocky; my second, although free from internal agony, was also strenuous. It was difficult to move, to reach the top of my hair to wash. I had to get creative with my body positions in order to allow the water to reach and rinse, and for my head to move closer towards my hands since my hands couldn't reach for my head. In doing so, I forgot the cardinal rule for hair washing: don't get shampoo in your eyes. It burned. *Shit!*

It was curious that after my drains were removed and I was able to gain back some of the things I had lost (ability to move, shower, and take deep breaths), I had my first emotional meltdown. Why was I crying *after* I just gained something back? It didn't make sense to me at the time. Later, I realized that my emotions were lagging in their recovery; or as my friend put it so eloquently, "When emotions rise in intensity following a trauma, it's because you're now safe to feel." I had been so focused on physical recovery that I hadn't paid an iota of attention to emotional recovery. I just cried and had no idea why I was crying.

The beginning of August quickly approached. Leona was going into first grade, and Sage was starting Kindergarten. I wanted to be able to take them to school to meet their teachers and find their classrooms. Although I shuffled at the pace of a sloth, I *was* moving and would find a way to make it happen.

School's Open House was on Tuesday; I had an appointment with Dr. Rehl to find out the lymph node biopsy results on Wednesday, and school started on Thursday. There were lots of big events and news happening in a tiny window of time. I was anxious for my lymph node report but ready to move on in my next step of recovery. All she had to do was tell me they were clear.

Token of Courage: Shift Your Perspective

There were many moments throughout my cancer-fighting journey that were traumatic. However, the memory of *that* surgery day, of those lights, of those sharp flesh-splicing tools, and of the terror that rolled through my body as I approached the room, were unparalleled. Those memories somehow haunted me long after I had reached the safety of solid ground, long after I had made it through to the other side of my storm.

In some ways they still do.

Ashley, my therapist, would tell me that we can't go back and rewrite our past. *Damn it*. We can't undo the things that have been done to us. She'd tell me that our histories are part of us, but they do not define us. Instead, we can reframe things in our minds and shift our perspective.

I'll be honest, I had no idea what the hell that looked like or how to go about doing it. It took me an entire year before I was finally able to experience this shift—at least in regards to that particular memory. Here's the best way I can describe it:

Imagine yourself standing in a field, watching some event unfold in front of you, when all of a sudden you shift your weight from your right leg to your left. You still see and hear the event in front of you, but it feels different.

I will never be able to undo this memory. It, along with the pain that followed, had been etched into my mind and left its stamp upon my soul; and although I may not be able to carve off this memory like the tumor itself, clarity can be gained with a new perspective.

When I shifted my weight from my right foot to my left, here's what I noticed. I saw how far we as a society have come; and I reckoned that it wasn't about what had happened to me, what I'd endured, or even what I'd lost; rather, it was about recognizing these things *could* happen to me in efforts to lengthen my life. It was about recognizing and appreciating what science and medicine could do for us now that it wasn't capable of doing in years prior. Then, it was about taking a second to ponder just how far we could go if we continued to push forward for a cure.

Another shift in perspective that changed everything for me and helped radical acceptance become that much more tangible was when I was challenged to think of that surgical room from my children's perspectives. It was about picking up their vision and looking at that operating room through their eyes. What would they see? Here is what I came up with—what I imagined they would say one day:

That room saved my mom's life. That room, that moment, was the start of healing my mom. That moment kicked off a journey that *my* mom took so that she could be here with me. I'm grateful for that room, and I'm proud of my mom and her courage to do all the scary things she did in order to stay here with me. My mom, she must really love me to have taken care of herself in that way."

Magic. These shifts were freaking magical. They didn't erase or change my past, or even my memories of it. I still have all of them. But reframing things helped to peel off a piece of trauma that had continued to haunt me. The memory of that moment—of that surgery—started to become part of me rather than define me.

Own your past: even those painful, dreaded moments that are much easier to deny. Know that those moments are only a part of you, they will *always* be a part of you, but that doesn't mean that you are forever bound by their iron chains. No! Those moments don't have to define you. Rather, they get folded in as part of the cake batter, part of your story, part of the woman that you are becoming—not the entirety of who you are. Don't try to deny your emotions or memories; rather, shift your weight from one foot to the next.

Chapter 9

The Buttons that Broke Me

Nugget of Knowledge

If you love to watch crime shows on TV, you're probably familiar with the word: *pathology*. But what exactly is pathology? What goes on behind the scenes? You may get a print out of your pathology, or have your provider translate the results, but there is so much that has to happen first in the heart of the lab in order to bring you that critical data.

Pathologists examine tissue samples to determine what is going on at the microscopic level. What secrets are held under the microscope? Is it cancer? If so, what kind? What grade? What is the *tumor's* pathology? Estrogen and progesterone status? What about HER2?

Pathologists are the hidden heroes of our cancer journeys. What they do and the data they gather provides surgeons, oncologists, and radiation oncologists with critical information used to determine the most appropriate treatment plans for our specific cancer. Without these diagnostic heroes working diligently behind the scenes, our healing from cancer would never take off. Patients who are triple positive, for example, will receive different care than those who are triple negative. Why? It's because their cancers are different and need to be destroyed in different ways. You have to know what you're fighting before you can wage a war.

So, what do these doctors do? Well, it's not like a vending

machine; you can't simply insert tissue samples and have them instantaneously spit out a report. There is great science at work in those labs; it's biology at its best, and it takes time and expertise to examine and diagnose disease.

On April 8th of 2020, I was afforded an incredible opportunity to do an interview for my podcast, *Keepers of the Flame*®, with a brilliant pathologist at Memorial Health University Medical Center, Dr. Charles T. Bruker. Dr. Bruker even took me on a tour of the pathology lab and walked me through what happens from surgery to slides to diagnosis.

While a patient is in surgery, the breast surgeon might do a sentinel node biopsy. The question that determines how the surgeon proceeds is whether or not cancer made it to that node. If the answer is yes, the surgeon may opt to do an axillary node dissection—where they remove all of the lymph nodes under that arm. If the answer is no, the surgeon can move on with the removal of the breast tissue. The sentinel lymph node is removed, and a nurse walks it next door to the fresh tissue lab where the pathologist immediately freezes the sample.

Once frozen, he slices the sample much like a meat slicer works in the deli. There's a sweet spot to how thin to make them because the thinner you slice them, the more slides get generated. Since this is all happening while the patient is under anesthesia, pathologists want to be efficient. Research shows that this 2mm thickness allows them to

Fig. 9. Pathologist Dr Bruker shows how fresh tissue samples are examined during surgery, March 2020

get a decent look at things without generating too many slides for that allotted time. After examining the fresh slides under the microscope, the pathologist phones the surgeon in the OR with the results.

Any of the other lymph nodes removed, along with the breast tissue itself, get sent to the lab where pathologists begin making permanent slides for further examination. They cannot make slides of the entire breast; that would yield an unruly number of slides, and all of that tissue isn't the target area. So, his team physically searches through a removed breast for the cancer. Much of this process involves a combination of science and art. They have to use their senses and know what they're feeling for.

Sometimes after a biopsy is done, physicians insert a clip to mark the spot that was biopsied. In the lab, these clips can often aid in locating the cancer. Another strategy they use is taking x-rays of the tissue; this aids in searching the tissue for any other concerning areas. They also have little one-inch trays that have the patient's data tagged on the edge. When tissue containing cancer is extracted from the specimen, it is placed in the little trays. A few other procedures are done, including running it through a tissue processor. Afterwards, these trays, each holding an individual sample cut from the specimen, are taken to embedding. The embedding machine sprays hot wax onto the sample in the tray, creating a block. This block can be sliced and used to

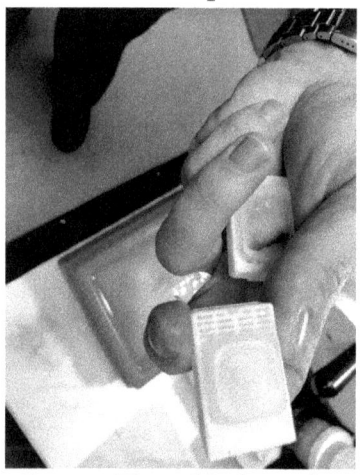

Fig. 10. Tissue blocks used in pathology, March 2020

make slides in a similar fashion to how the fresh tissue slides were made.

A different machine is used to determine the estrogen and progesterone status, which is critical information for treatment. An antibody of estrogen is applied to one of the slides and then the machine does its thing. The same is done for progesterone. HER2 status can be determined in this manner if it is strongly positive or negative. If the HER2 is in the middle zone, they do another procedure.

Fig. 11. My cancer slides and learning how to examine them with Dr. Bruker, March 2020

Next, all of these slides are taken to the pathologist where the cellular activity is studied. We were able to look up my cancer slides, go to the "card catalog," and take my slides to the microscope. I was fortunate enough to have Dr. Bruker let me look for myself, and he explained what we were seeing and what pathologists looked for.

Breast cancer comes in many varieties, characterized by location, size, lymph node involvement, hormone and HER2 status, as well as something called the *grade*. (This is different from the cancer stage). The tumor grade is assessed based on three criteria: tubule formation, nuclear grade, and mitotic rate. Tumors with a high grade (2-3) are typically more aggressive; low grade (or 1) are less aggressive. The tumor grade is based on how wonky those cancer cells look in comparison to normal breast tissue cells. Mine was a grade 3—crazy cancer boogers.

When cells have gone sour and are not behaving properly, they look oblong and stacked next to one another—like flat sardines trying to mimic sedimentary rock. (That's my description…but essentially, they're not looking like normal cells). This is called tubule formation. Pathologists also identify the nuclear grade by looking to see if the nuclei of the cells are oversized. Also, how deformed is that nuclear envelope? In my cells, I saw some giant nuclei and some struggling envelopes.

What about mitotic rate? Mitosis is cell division; this happens all the time with our somatic cells. We want mitosis in healthy cells, but not when those cells are cancerous. The more mitotic figures captured on the slides, the higher the grade. I was able to see evidence of mitosis happening in several of my cells.

There is an amazing world of biology happening in our bodies: in all of our bodies, those with and without cancer. To see what's happening with cells inside your tissues is quite miraculous. Doing what pathologists do—studying, examining and diagnosing from this microscopic level—is not only genius, it's a vital step in saving your life.

Personal Voyage

Bryan and I went to meet with Dr. Rehl to review the results from my tissue's pathology. We were escorted to the same exam room where I had received the orange mega binder and was told I had cancer and needed a mastectomy. Neither of us were fans of that damn room, and although my gut whispered that something wasn't quite right, I remained mildly optimistic. Perhaps I put on my humorous, numbing armor. If I could find humor and be hopeful, then surely I had the strength to handle anything that was thrown my way.

Time slowed to a near standstill while we waited for Dr.

Rehl. Sixty seconds makes one minute on any normal given day, but it's a fucking lie when it comes to waiting for life-altering news. Ten minutes, five minutes…even two minutes…it doesn't matter. They all feel like an eternity. Finally, Dr. Rehl entered: Here was the moment of truth. I knew it was bad news if cancer made it to the lymph nodes. That meant chemo. That meant there was a distinct possibility that the cells had relocated, and they could be secretly hiding anywhere in my body. *Okay, deep breaths. Let the woman speak.*

We didn't get the news we had hoped for. My gut whispers were right: some slippery, fast cells didn't waste any time and made it to the lymph nodes. This didn't mean the cancer cells had left the station and set up camp somewhere else, but then again, they could have. All it took was one stubborn ass cell to have made a move, and there was no way to know for certain.

Chemotherapy was recommended. Dr. Rehl had already put the referral in and set up the appointment for 11:00 that same morning in Savannah with the medical oncologist, Dr. Spellman. She explained that if the cancer didn't show up at all in the lymph nodes, we would do hormone therapy. If the cancer was 2mm in size, we would be doing chemo without question. However, I was in the gray area. I had a micromet; my lymph node involvement was 1mm in size, about the size of a period on a sheet of paper. She explained this was where oncologists would differ in their recommendations.

When in the gray area, some oncologists would wait until they received the oncotype results to make their decision. Others would make a recommendation after weighing all parameters: age, health, type of cancer, etc. Dr. Spellman took into consideration all of my personal health factors, and for me, she recommended that it was best to hit my cancer with all tools available. Chemotherapy would be part of my personal arsenal. I was young and healthy enough to withstand chemo, and the risks of treatment did not outweigh the gains for me. I agreed.

I wasn't excited to have chemo, but I wanted those renegade cells to be killed! I didn't want any chance of them hiding in my brain, liver, bone...anywhere. They were not welcome in my body; so yeah, if my body could take it and it was in my best interest, then chemo the fuck out of them!

I would have four rounds of chemotherapy, one round every three weeks. They would give me a combination treatment of Taxotere and Cytoxan, and I would start in about three weeks since I was still healing from my mastectomy. I was told that I was going to lose my hair. Oddly, this upset me more than losing my breasts.

After chemo and reconstruction, which would slow down pending white blood cell count, they would take my ovaries. This cancer was taking everything: my breasts, my hair, my ovaries, my time, my patience, my health, my sense of safety in the world. Still, I was determined that it wouldn't take me from my family! I was pissed, ready to kick cancer to the curb. *What if I had not done genetic testing? Thank God I had been put on this path now rather than later!* I clung tightly to that blessing despite this punch-me-in-the-gut setback.

We were emotionally weary and weak after receiving this second blow. The war wasn't over. The first hurdle had been cleared: my mastectomy. But this was only the beginning. I had another hurdle ahead of me, and I had to find the strength to armor up.

My friend's mom, Kim, brought us dinner that night. I stood on the front porch talking with her for a while; we laughed some and cried some more. When I relayed the diagnosis and the size of the unwelcomed beasts within my lymph nodes (about the size of a period), without missing a beat she asked, "Well, what size font were they talking?"

Somehow through watery eyes, I felt the corners of my mouth slip into a smile as laughter found its way to ring out from within me. We laughed some more. She gave me a hug and held me tight as she comforted and prayed for me.

I told her I was worried about losing my hair. I was afraid it would frighten my girls, that hearing the word *cancer* and seeing my bald head would make them think I was in danger of dying. I didn't want to shatter any stability in their world; I wanted to protect them from unnecessary fear. Perhaps I was even afraid of thinking the same. I was fighting for my life, but I was afraid of facing my mortality.

My friend's mom told me what a beautiful lesson in compassion this would be for my girls. They would have an opportunity at an early age to learn kindness, to not judge those who were different, to know that everyone was going through something you knew nothing about, and that love and compassion towards all people was essential to embracing the light of our humanity. Those lessons were powerful ones; they were ones that I wanted more than anything to impart to my children. I appreciated being reminded of this and for being shown yet another opportunity for greatness to rise from the shadows.

School started at the beginning of August, and although I had made great strides since my mastectomy, I was still weak and moving slowly. I got exhausted easily, but I was adamant that I would walk my two girls into school on their first day, even if Leona's classroom was at the end of the longest hall.

We took a family photo that morning, then loaded up the

van with two eager children and all of their fresh supplies. When the bell rang, we dropped Sage off at her kindergarten class and then walked the length of the never-ending hallway to Leona's first grade room. We gave the girls hugs and kisses, took a few pictures, and said our goodbyes. I was proud of them; they were growing so fast, and I was excited for what this school year could bring them. I was also proud of myself for being able to share this moment with them. After all, getting ready in the morning still took me well over an hour.

Fig. 12. Family photo on the first day of school, August 3, 2017

I had a few emotional snags while the girls were in school that first day. The first one was scheduling my portacath placement surgery. I needed it for chemotherapy, and I was told that it was best to go ahead and have it placed so the wound could heal before my first treatment. The portacath would be sewn beneath my skin and used in lieu of an IV to administer the toxins.

I picked the kids up from school and went through their book bags to locate their homework, paperwork required for me to fill out, etc. I was hanging on by a thread at this point, fatigued from pushing myself too hard, and emotionally weary from my latest cancer setback. Still, in spite of my fatigue, I was determined to complete my first-day-of-school duties.

This is when I found the note…a note that tipped me over the edge. I received this distressing, curt note from a teacher on the very first day of school. It was about buttons. *Are you fucking kidding me? Buttons?* They knew what our family was going through at home, yet of all children to single out it had to be mine.

In our district, students were required to wear uniforms. There were multiple ensembles students could choose from, but the handbook outlined the expectations. Leona and Sage each wore the exact same dress. It was a style that Leona wore every week the previous year, one that faculty's children wore, and one that multiple girls across the entire district wore as well. But on day one, a yellow sticky note accompanied *my* child home.

"Mr. & Mrs. Williams, Good afternoon! Unfortunately, only 2 or 3 button polo style shirts are uniform approved. Leona's top is not considered approved. Thanks."

I lost my shit.

I held it together through my mastectomy, through being told that I needed chemo, and then I lost my shit over buttons.

I cried for over an hour about buttons. My child's wardrobe was being picked to pieces over the number of buttons on her shirt! Furthermore, what the hell was wrong with her dress? The white built-in collar only had two fucking buttons on it anyway, which met the requirement for appropriate fucking button-ship.

After my meltdown, I picked myself up and went to the Parent Teacher Handbook. If our wardrobe was going to be scrutinized each day with a fine-tooth comb, then I would dedicate just as much diligence to the contract to ensure that the clothes my children wore to school were in compliance. They were.

As much as I despised confrontation, I was not going to let my children be singled out. I wrote a response where I reminded them that "nowhere in the dress code description did it specify the number of buttons allowed on a shirt. It only specified how many buttons could be unbuttoned in the General Standards Section—bullet two. Therefore, I do not understand how Leona's outfit could be considered not approved." I even went as far as to scrutinize a misplaced comma that actually granted permission for either collared *or* polo shirts, allowing for *any* number of buttons on the shirt.

I never liked confrontation, and as a former teacher, I respected how hard faculty and staff worked daily. I loved our district, our schools, and the faculty were phenomenal educators. I wanted to be the parent who spoiled and helped teachers in any way they needed. So, it gave me great angst to send that letter. I knew it would brand me as *that* parent. Still, it wasn't right. I felt like my kids were singled out; and honestly, I was pissed that while I was facing my mortality and terrified of leaving my girls motherless, this teacher picked on my child over something as trivial as buttons.

As I was getting ready that morning, I saw my scars in the mirror, and for the first time, I didn't hate them. I didn't fall to pieces with grief over my maimed body that day. I stared at my wounds in the mirror, noticed the rawness, the pain, the way my skin pulled together like fabric and thread. I saw the dried blood, the glue, and the tenderness of it all. I saw the absence of my former self, and though I felt the pain and heartache gripping my soul, I did not cry. As I stared at them this particular morning, I did not hold hatred and resentment toward my unfathomable wounds. Rather, they reminded me that sometimes in this world there were things worth fighting for. My girls would always be at the top of my list! I would fight for my kids, for the battles both large and small. I would continue to fight like hell for my life and, as needed, I would also stand up for them on issues as minute as buttons.

My scars seemed to transform into badges, reminding me of all that I held dear, and I couldn't hate my scars or the lessons they taught me.

My aunt made me a hat with buttons that once belonged to my grandmother, and I chuckled every time I wore it. Perhaps it was because it stroked my inner feistiness. It was a subtle message: *I'm facing death, I am afraid, yet life and these little ebbs and flows are only part of the journey, and I am still journeying.* It was a reminder of battles large and small, and the hat itself comforted me with the touch from family both present and departed.

My port placement surgery was approaching, and I knew I needed to address this with Leona and Sage. They would most certainly see my portacath, and they would definitely notice when Mom was bald. I was nervous about breaking this news to them.

I had not yet used the *cancer* word, and I was frightened that somehow my children would grow fearful from hearing the forbidden word. There was no getting around it, though. They needed to know what was going on, and they needed to hear it from me.

I fixed them each lunch and sat down with them for a picnic in the family room. I asked them if I had ever told them the name of the booboo the doctors had taken away. They told me no, so I continued to tell them that the name of my booboo was cancer.

"Have you ever heard of that before?" I asked.

They shook their heads no, and I took a sigh of relief.

"Well, there are lots of different kinds of cancer, and they're usually named for where they're found. Since mine was in my breast, they called it breast cancer." *So far, so good.* I swallowed and made myself keep going.

"Doctors took Mommy's breast cancer, my booboo, away. But they want to make sure that it never comes back. To do this they want to give Mommy some special medicine called chemo. They have to give Mommy this medicine at the hospital, and they give it to me through a special door." I paused to see if they were following me and then quickly reviewed.

"Mommy had a booboo called?"

They answered, "Breast cancer."

"And they want to give me medicine called?"

"Chemo," they replied.

"Good, and how will they give it to me?"

"With a magic door."

"That's right, and they call this door a port."

I continued on, "Sometimes medicine could have side effects, and this kind might make Mommy tired for a few days. It's also gonna cause Mommy to lose her hair."

I tried to hide my internal wince. I was bracing for the fear to rise in them, much like it had already done inside of me.

"I'm gonna look like Unc (my Uncle) for a little while, but afterwards, my hair will grow back, and you can both help me pick out new hairstyles as it grows longer."

They were quiet, processing this strange, new information.

"Do you girls have any questions?"

Sage said, "Yes. Mommy, can we please have some more chips?"

I exhaled in relief.

"Sure, baby. No problem."

I kissed them both and told them that if they thought of any questions, anything at all, I'd be there to answer them.

*   *   *

While I waited for the time to come for chemotherapy, Dr. Spellman's office was working on securing insurance approval. One evening I got a call from the lab that would be doing the oncotype test: the test that would determine how successful chemo would be in fighting my cancer. The lab informed me that our insurance would not cover the test, that it was deemed "genetic testing." The lab continued to tell me that we would be responsible for $4,620 out of pocket and then asked, "Would you care to continue with the test?" *Wait, what?* I wanted to call my insurance first.

It was the most absurd thing because I had received a letter from my insurance company explaining that they were denying me chemotherapy treatment prior to obtaining the results to this oncotype test, which *they were refusing to cover!* This didn't make any sense, especially since they had already approved my port placement. *Why the hell would you approve a port only to deny chemo?*

One round of chemo could easily be over $11,000, and I needed four rounds. The insurance needed to pay for it; they just needed some clarity from the provider. So, I picked up the phone, called my provider, and got connected with a fabulous young woman named Kia.

Kia was my hero! She first had me take a deep breath and then laughed with me at this ridiculous situation created by the insurance company. Then, she gave me her cell phone number and stepped outside to talk with me some more. Kia took on my problems as if they were her own. She said that she would make my case her first priority that day, and she would go all the way up to the insurance commissioner if need be. She reassured me that they couldn't deny me lifesaving care over a test they didn't cover.

I let go of control, passed my stress off to Kia, and let her work on it. A few days later, she called me with great news. Insurance had approved treatment. I later got the results of the oncotype test and reviewed them with the oncologist. My score was a 29, which translated to: It was a damn good thing I was doing chemotherapy. The score indicated that my tumor was more aggressive, but it would respond very well to treatment. Dr. Spellman also told me that after treatment was finished, my risk of recurrence would be less than 10%. I had a plan; I had a first chemo date. I needed to plow through this next chapter, and then I'd be closer to putting this mess behind me.

Token of Courage: Revise Your Plan

Life doesn't always follow the outlines we design for ourselves. When the bitter wind blows those blueprints right out of the window and down the street, skipping away like leaves on a brisk fall day, don't panic and chase after them. Instead, take a deep breath…and say, "Damn, that sucks."

Once you've acknowledged that the original plans are lost, you sit your butt back down at the drafting table to create a plan B. Pivot. Revise. What can you do now? What can you still salvage? How can you adjust? Does this change your overall goal? Or does it merely alter the benchmarks along the way? Can you create new beauty within this plan? Can you find a way to thread hope throughout this outline?

Stay flexible and adjust your expectations of how much of the plan is in your control. Do what you can do when you can do it, and let go and have faith in others when you can do that too. Speaking with my kids about something difficult, braving another surgery for my port, taking charge and chopping the length off of my hair, and raising hell with the insurance company were all things that I *could* do. Letting go and trusting in the medical staff that sliced open my body once more and trusting in Kia to tackle my insurance snag as if it were her life on the line took just as much courage as the things that I did for myself.

Revisions take courage, and making them is token #9. It takes courage to make changes and pivot when necessary, especially when we've become attached to how we think life will go.

Chapter 10

Drip by Drip

Nugget of Knowledge

Some patients are given chemotherapy prior to surgery, others afterwards. Either way, chemotherapy is a systemic treatment, meaning the drugs spread throughout the entire body. I was fortunate enough to have the opportunity to interview Vanessa Brink, a NP in medical oncology, for one of my podcast episodes, and she used the metaphor of a tornado when talking about chemotherapy. She said that having chemotherapy was like having a tornado run through your body. Tornados may come and go quickly, but the damage that's left in their wake and the repair required to move on with normalcy takes time and a great deal of work (Williams 2020, Episode 39).

Chemo drugs are in and out of your body within a few hours; and you can even see this with Adriamycin, or more commonly referred to as The Red Devil. It is a bright red chemo drug, and patients actually pee bright red while it's still in their system, however it exits their body after a few hours. According to Vanessa, even though the drugs move quickly, that internal tornado wreaked havoc, and consequently, your body requires time and a lot of work to repair that damage. Fatigue may set in as your body's way of protecting you. It's indicative of your body focusing its energy on repairing the damage and healing you from the inside.

In our interview, Vanessa encourages patients to be completely honest and forthcoming with their oncologist. Some people are afraid to speak up and tell their doctors about certain pain, discomfort, or side effects because they're afraid of getting some form of inferior treatment if they can't "hack it." But here's the thing that Vanessa wanted patients to know: The initial dosage is determined based on height and weight alone. However, every person's body chemistry is different, along with what they've been through, how their cancer behaves, and how their body responds.

Your oncologist will give you the best possible treatment for you and your cancer, but they can only do that if you're honest about what you're experiencing. Tweaking your infusion dosage does not equate to lessening the quality. On the contrary, it allows them to better meet your needs.

Breast cancer patients are often given what they call a combination treatment. This means you receive two transfusions. If you think back to your high school biology class, a cell's life cycle consists of interphase (including the G1, S, and G2 phases) and cell division (which includes mitosis and cytokinesis). Basically, a cell grows, replicates its DNA, gears up for mitosis, and then separates into two identical diploid daughter cells.

The different chemotherapy drugs target cells at different points in that cell division process; so, when you use a combination of chemo drugs, you're maximizing the number of cells affected, thus increasing the overall effectiveness of your infusions (Williams 2020, Episode 39).

Still, one of the casualties of chemotherapy is a reduction in your white blood cell (WBC) count. White blood cells are produced in the bone marrow and are part of your body's immune system. They help fight off any unwelcome bug that accosts your body; and since chemo has the unwanted side effect of walloping your white blood cell count, oncologists follow your counts closely and may even prescribe medicines, such as the Neulasta shot, to go into the bone marrow and jump start WBC production.

Even still, this is why cancer patients are susceptible to other illnesses: like the common cold, the flu, and so on. Under normal circumstances, cancer patients may have been able to fight off these viruses, but under active treatment you become immunocompromised and can get really ill from so much as a common cold.

Chemo brain is another common side effect of chemotherapy. Although it can range wildly from one patient to the next, it's often described by survivors as this cognitive fog. This can manifest as forgetting important dates or having difficulty finding the right word.

Personal Voyage

I finally achieved enough range of motion in my arms and torso to be able to drive again. It had been nearly a month, and with this renewed freedom, I felt like a teenager all over again. However, I was still sporting my satin pillow and was *not* setting out on adolescent adventures.

It was during this time that I also decided that it might be a good idea to cut my hair. I thought that it might be worth getting used to having my hair off of my neck before it all fell out with chemo. I was hopeful that this would be less traumatic for me. Baby steps could ease me into acceptance of the inevitable. So, one of my friend's moms accompanied me to the salon, and

I had my long hair chopped off to chin length. It wasn't a haircut that I was excited for; I liked being able to have a ponytail. However, I had to say goodbye to my hair regardless, and at least this let me do it in stages.

It was the summer of the great solar eclipse. We lived right outside of Savannah, and we were going to have a near totality solar eclipse on August 21, 2017. It was a once in a lifetime opportunity, and everyone was getting

Fig. 13. Learning to drive again, August 2017

excited for it. It was also two days before my first chemotherapy, and both Bryan's parents and my mom came to help.

At my first appointment, I was determined and petrified all in the same breath. Bryan came with me, and I was shuffled to the lab where they pricked my finger and stole more blood to check my white blood cell count prior to it getting sucker punched. Next, they took me to vitals, followed by an exam room since Dr. Spellman wanted to meet with me prior to receiving the first set of cocktails.

Next up was the treatment room. It was a giant room with recliner chairs in rows. Patients were resting in these chairs, draped with blankets, and hooked up to IVs that pumped various chemicals into their bodies. There was one recliner left, and Bryan pulled up a regular chair next to mine. The nurses came to introduce themselves and get me started. I would be there for two to three hours while the poisons trickled into my body. They prepped my portacath, stabbed it with the IV, and started the process. Cytoxin and Taxotere took turns flooding my veins, yet so far, I didn't feel too badly.

After the last drop of chemicals had entered my body, the nurse came over to unhook me. She also set me up on Neulasta, which came in the form of a battery-operated sticker to wear on my arm, which would jump start my production of white blood cells. When the Neulasta was first applied to my arm, there was a series of beeps followed by ticking and then a BAM. The BAM was when the needle flicked into my skin. It felt like a giant rubber band snapped on my arm. But to me, it was not nearly as bad as when they pricked my finger for blood. My surgery had left me quite fearful of needles.

Walking, drinking water, and resting were the three things I insisted on doing for self-care. Vanessa had noted in our interview that patients who responded best were those who got up, moved around, and did something. Rest was certainly good, but there was something to be said for not lying in bed all day.

The Neulasta was set to go off about 28 hours after treatment. I had completely forgotten about my cool, new sticker and was perplexed when I heard beeping. I was chasing my tail around the kitchen, searching for what alarm was going off. The noise soon stopped, so I sat down at the kitchen table to work on something. Then, I heard this ticking noise and couldn't figure out why my digital watch was making noise. Finally, it dawned on me that my battery-operated sticker had just detonated.

Luckily, I never got sick from treatment. I just felt incredibly worn down, like how you feel right before you get sick. Occasionally, I'd get a little nauseated but it was never severe enough to warrant anti-nausea medicine. I did, however, experience intense bone pain. I chalked this up as a good thing because it meant that the Neulasta was working. It was going deep into my bone marrow to force the production of white blood cells. Sometimes, it was crippling and had me stuck in the bed. I hated not being able to move.

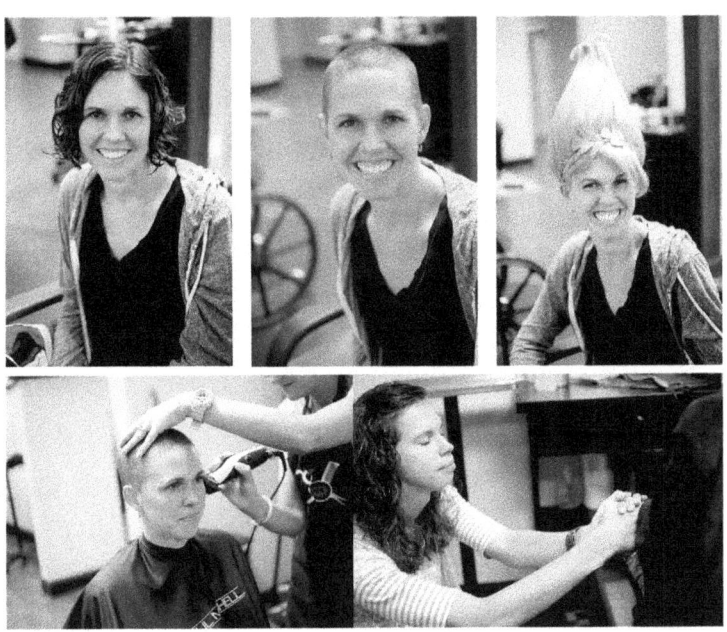

Fig. 14. Joyce having her head shaved on August 26, 2017.
Photographs by Tonya Perry.

Two of my friends accompanied me to the hair salon the Saturday after my first chemo. I was incredibly anxious about losing my hair, but I didn't have a choice in the matter. It was going to fall out in a few weeks anyway, and I'd rather it be removed on my terms than fall out in chunks on my pillow. I knew it would destroy me if it came out in gobs everywhere. I wanted to have at least an ounce of control over what was happening to my body. So I made an appointment to have my hair stylist shave my hair for me. I cried the whole time.

My aunt made hats for chemo patients out of really soft yarn, and she started me on a new fashion kick. She sent me dozens of hats to wear, to donate, etc. After my head was shaved, my two friends and I each wore a hat and went to lunch. It was an emotionally exhausting day.

Sage's fifth birthday arrived at the end of August, and although I was dealing with my own struggles, I refused to let that take away from her day. I had already planned ahead and booked the painting studio in town. I had also ordered a Princess Poppy wig for myself and a Branch wig for Bryan. We were the family of *Trolls*. I loved the movie almost as much as Leona and Sage did. The messages in it spoke to me—not giving up, finding happiness and being optimistic, leaning on friends when needed, and picking yourself up and bringing about change (Dorn and Mitchell 2016). Even though life wasn't always cupcakes and rainbows, the songs "Get Back up Again" (Kendrick 2016) and "True Colors" (Kendrick and Timberlake 2016) seemed to be my newest theme songs.

This birthday party was a welcomed distraction. It made my heart warm and happy knowing I was able to find a way, despite all that was going on, to help bring that birthday magic on Sage's special day.

September 23, 2017 was my second round of chemo, 50% of the way to the finish line. This time, Bryan stayed home to manage the

Fig. 15. Sage's fifth birthday party celebrated at Paint and Possibilities in August 2017

girls and their schedules while my mom accompanied me to the hospital. It was more or less the same routine: Get your finger pricked, meet with the oncologist, and find a recliner to hang out in while the drugs dripped.

Fig. 16. Joyce snuggled with her girls after chemo, September 2017

Mom and I played cards to pass the time, and then afterwards, we went to get a jump start on Christmas shopping. My symptoms also followed the same pattern as round one. I was fine the day of treatment, but I was exhausted for two days afterwards, followed by two days of intense bone pain.

A new symptom soon developed: I lost my taste. It was the weirdest thing. If you looked at my tongue, the taste buds looked fried. They didn't lay flat like normal; they appeared as if they had tried out some new spiky hairdo and sat straight up. My taste returned about a week later, just in time for the next round of chemo.

Michelle started a new business selling nail polish that you peeled and stuck on your nails like stickers. She spoiled me by doing my nails with the breast cancer awareness polish. I know it seems silly, but I loved my manicure. Seeing these pretty pink nails on my fingers reminded me of my femininity despite all that cancer had taken from me. My boobs were gone, my hair was gone, and I was feeling like a shell of the woman that I once was. It was kind of childish for me to lean on something as simple as nail polish, but I swear this pretty pink-ribboned manicure reminded me of the beauty and strength that I had

Fig. 17. Joyce with breast cancer awareness nail polish, September 2017

within. I was more than my hair, more than my nails, more than my boobs; I was me, and that ought to be enough. A simple thing like pink nails helped me hold tight to that truth.

October 4th, 2017, was the day of my third chemotherapy treatment. My parents were determined to be there for me again. They drove down the day prior, and my dad accompanied me the next morning to my third round of treatment. We left the house early enough to get to Savannah in time to sneak a quick breakfast in at Waffle House. I enjoyed hanging out with my dad. We talked a little bit about everything: my cancer, stories from his youth, strategies for financial planning, our shared lack of spatial sense.

I was becoming an expert at the chemo shuffle: finger prick, vitals, doctor, recliner, then sit and wait. Daddy and I played gin while the drugs took turns flooding my system. I wish I could have blamed chemo brain for not winning gin, but my dad is brilliant. He can remember every card that has been played; I didn't stand a chance. Still, we laughed and had fun in each other's company. I do think it's important to bring something to your infusions that brings you a sliver of joy. It could be playing cards, a friend to read to you, a playlist of empowering, you-are-a-badass kinda songs…anything. Warm socks, journals, crochet or knitting, joke books, and puzzles are also great ideas to consider.

My symptoms followed their regular pattern yet again: tired for two days, bone pain for the next two, lost sense of taste, and another emotional pitfall. I had to force myself to do things: be with friends, go on walks, write. Later, a new symptom layered on top of the others. My eyes started leaking. Dry eyes were supposedly a symptom of chemo, and they hit me after chemo number three. Water welled up in my eyes. Unlike regular tears that roll down your cheek when you blink, these little nuggets stayed and blurred my vision.

Sage came down with strep, but when I took her to urgent care for confirmation with a throat swab, she did not want to cooperate. I couldn't afford to get sick on chemo, and I knew I was at risk. With my white blood cells struggling, a sickness could have sent me to the hospital or jeopardized treatment… or both.

As a mom, I wanted my baby girl to feel better. Yet, I couldn't force a five-year-old to say "ah" for that highly unpleasant swab, and bribery didn't work. She flat-out refused to do the test. She was scared and crying; I was frustrated. I left there unable to know for certain about Sage and with the added freaking cherry on top: I was told to be careful because they had positive flu tests done in this very room earlier that day. *Great!* I then took Sage to her pediatrician, and they managed to do the throat swab. It was confirmed: I had been exposed to both strep and the flu. *Lord, help my immune system!*

October 25, 2017 was my very last round. *Hallelujah!* Bryan took the day off of work to manage the kids' schedules, and my best friend, Michelle, came with me to keep me company during treatment. I gave myself a continuous pep talk: *I've got this!* I also tried to encourage myself with thoughts about my hair soon returning. *When my hair grows back after this round, it'll be growing back to stay!* I actually was quite excited for the day that I would have to shave my legs once more. That would be one hell of a happy nuisance, and I would welcome it with a fresh bottle of shaving cream and a shiny new razor. I'd never again complain about a bad hair day either; when that day came, I'd smile and chuckle and love that I could have a bad hair day because I'd actually have hair again. I couldn't wait for those moments.

When I met with the oncologist, she told me that I'd never be rid of her. From now until forever, I'd have follow-ups with her office. I suppose it was a good thing that they would keep tabs on me, despite being forever branded as a cancer patient. I wanted them to watch me; I wanted to be sure that cancer *never* returned.

I set a date to have my port flushed, and the doctor told me that in January we would discuss the medicine that I'd be required to take for five years. It was a hormone blocker, and a potential side effect was depression. The removal of my ovaries would have the same side effect. It felt like I was handed two more petri dishes where my sadness could multiply.

Three surgeons and a genetic counselor had all advised me to have my ovaries removed because of my BRCA2 mutation. With it, I was twenty times more likely than the average woman to get ovarian cancer. Also, my cancer was hormone-fed, and the overachieving mutant cells had made a fast dash to the lymph nodes in the first place.

Bryan and I met with the gynecologic oncologist to discuss yet another surgery. I took comfort in knowing that this surgeon was the best in his field. Still, I left his office with both relief and terror. It was a weird combination of emotions. I was relieved to have answers. He said they would be able to perform the hysterectomy and the switch out portion of my reconstruction at the same time. This would mean that two of my surgeries could be done under the same anesthesia. This meant there would only be *one* recovery period! Furthermore, he would be able to perform the surgery laparoscopically. This was the least invasive method, would have minimal blood loss, and would make my recovery period shorter.

Still, this surgery would throw me into an immediate onset of surgically-induced menopause; and God only knew how my body would handle the loss of estrogen. The normal progression of menopause happened gradually; however, I would be suffering a cold turkey loss of the hormones that, in some regards, defined my persona. How would my mood, emotions, and physical body withstand this instantaneous deficit?

They set my surgery date for December 7th, which was great for both insurance purposes (we'd already met our out of pocket max) and for wrapping up a rather difficult year. I'd say goodbye to 2017 and hello to a brand new year. With this surgery date and where I was in my current cancer fight, this meant I could be done with cancer by Christmas!

Unfortunately, my relief and excitement were paired equally with trepidation and fear. The surgeon proceeded to inform me that there was a 3-10% chance that cancer was already in my ovaries. Of course, we wouldn't know this until after surgery when they biopsied everything. I knew these odds were low, but when you just survived hell and you're told you might have to endure more, optimism takes a back seat for a few minutes.

He told me we'd hope cancer wasn't there (no shit), and that he'd "be honest" and let me know that ovarian cancer wasn't as easily treated as breast cancer. He said that it liked to reoccur, even with the ovaries removed (son-of-a-bitch cells). If the biopsy concluded the presence of cancer cells, I would undoubtedly require more chemo. Then, he continued to discuss what else I'd have to endure, but all that I heard from that point onward was Charlie Brown's teacher talking and a loop of trivia: *70-80% of women diagnosed with late stage ovarian cancer would die from it* (Chilkov 2025).

So, there I stood once more at the entrance to a dark, crappy tunnel. There were a lot of unknowns and things that I couldn't control, which seriously pissed me off, and I didn't have all of my answers mapped out in front of me. However, not doing the surgery and burying my head in the sand would not fix this problem for me. I had to summon my courage and brave yet another battle. I prayed for peace and guidance and cancer-free biopsies. I let optimism ride shotgun once more, despite fear gripping the steering wheel.

Token of Courage: Get Back Up Again

Many people told me I was optimistic, and for the most part I was—especially in the beginning before my giant rumbles of unruly emotions. I had always aimed to look for the light in the dark, no matter how dismal. It was part of who I had always been and who I wanted to be. I was a happy, positive person.

Truthfully, I may have craved strength and positivity, but I did not always embody them. I had my meltdowns too. Big, red, puffy face, tears running down, feeling like I'd been hit in the gut and stripped of any hope…hardly able to move. Yet somehow in my mind I equated sadness with weakness, and I never wanted to show it.

I wanted to lead by example and naively thought that to be a good example I had to remain strong, happy, and unwavering in my determination at all times. However, those are not realistic expectations, and the better example to set is allowing others to see that it's okay to cry, it's okay to feel like crap, it's okay to fail, and it's okay to fall to pieces. It's the rising up afterwards that matters more.

In life there will inevitably be some sort of trial that makes you feel lost, alone, and too weak to rise. I found mine. But, whatever your struggles are, you'll move forward too, even if you don't know how. Courage token #10: Get back up again; and while on the rise, recognize that there's no shame in having fallen in the first place. It sucks, but it doesn't mean you're weak. It means you're alive.

Chapter 11

The Landscape of Loss

Nugget of Knowledge

Grief accompanies loss, and all of us will experience some form of loss in our lives. It is part of living. However, grief is not exclusively linked to the loss of a loved one. Breast cancer and the treatments that follow come with an abundant amount of loss. We experience the loss of health, loss of our sense of self, loss of body parts, loss of feeling feminine with the removal of organs or loss of hormones, loss of hair, loss of fingernails, loss of feeling the sensation of touch on our breasts, loss of our sense of safety or direction, and loss of control.

The five stages of grief, according to Elisabeth Kubler-Ross, are denial, anger, bargaining, depression, and acceptance (Counselman-Carpenter and Redcay 2020). My work with Ashley taught me these stages aren't always sequential, and you can revisit the stages throughout your grief process.

Denial can be expressed by people in a variety of ways. They may pretend nothing is wrong, ignore it, refuse to talk about it, or practice avoidance in other ways…perhaps by keeping insanely busy, which was my go-to strategy. Anger arises when we're forced to accept the unavoidable and are left wondering, "Why me?" (Counselman-Carpenter and Redcay 2020). Bargaining is the idea of pleading with someone, perhaps a higher power, with "if I do this, will you please help me escape from that?" Depression is that overwhelming wave of sadness and hopelessness that hits when you realize this is happening to you and you cannot escape it. Acceptance is when you come to terms with what is happening and acknowledge that it is part of your story.

A friend shared a TED talk with me about neurogenesis in adults. Of course, as a biology girl and a cancer patient, I was intrigued. The speaker was a neuroscientist, and his friend, an oncologist, was puzzled that some of his patients who had been cured of cancer developed symptoms of depression. *Why, if you are cured, would you be sad?* According to the neuroscientist, it made sense. The drugs given to patients to kill off the cancer cells also attacked other cells: skin, hair, and neurons. The hippocampus in the brain is responsible for memory and mood; so, it made sense that if the drugs affected these neurons, it was also plausible that chemo could have been contributing to sadness on a cellular level (Thuret 2015).

Acknowledging and naming your emotions are among the first steps towards tending to your emotional health. Siegel & Bryson in *The Whole-Brain Child* say that you must, "Name it to tame it." In order to process through and address an overwhelming emotion, you must first be able to simply notice it…give it a name.

Gloria Wilcox designed a feelings wheel to assist with this. It's color coordinated and divided into the primary emotions: anger, fear, sadness, joy, and so on. From the center outward, these primary emotions utilized new words that are variants of that main emotion. For example, fear and its color realm might include variants such as: helpless, anxious, insecure, worried, frightened, terrified, and overwhelmed. The idea is that when we increase our emotional vocabulary, when we are able to adequately acknowledge and express our emotional experiences, we can begin to address and manage them. It's even okay if all you can express in any given moment is, "Hey, I'm in the red today."

In *Working with Grief & Traumatic Loss: Theory, Practice, Personal Reflection, and Self-Care* (2020), Elisabeth Counselman-Carpenter and Alex Recay explain different exercises that you can do to help work through grief and process trauma. One activity mentioned is the control/no control circle. On a sheet of paper, draw a giant circle, and inside of it write all of the things that you can actually control, while writing all of the things that you can't control outside of the circle. I might write outside the circle: time, when I die, the fact that I was diagnosed with cancer, whether or not my children inherited my BRCA2 mutation, fear, triggers, how other people respond, and so on. While on the inside of the circle, I might write: gather information, go to doctor appointments, move forward with treatment, spend time with my family, call a counselor.

Once you have your circle drawn and filled out, imagine crumpling up all of those things outside of your circle of control and picture sending them in a box up to a higher power or watching it float away on a cloud. Next, switch your attention back to the circle of control and focus on *those* things. *This is all I can ask of myself right now.*

Personal Voyage

In the midst of my own personal storm, I often felt hopeless and swallowed up by grief, like a surge of emotional waves were trying to shake me off my raft. Yes, there were times when my strength actually surprised the crap out of me. But there were other times when I felt the quicksand rising up to my neck. Emotions bubbled up and spilled all over the place, despite my attempts to shove that shit back in the bag. I seriously thought if I ignored my negative emotions, they'd just go away. Denial.

I honestly didn't know how to handle them. They didn't follow a step-by-step action plan, and they were more intense than I'd ever known. If fear, sadness, and grief were like gentle waves prior to cancer, after diagnosis they blasted over me like a freaking tsunami. They picked me up, dumped me in the deepest, darkest part of the ocean somewhere, and then did an alligator roll to ensure I was truly panicked and in over my head.

Emotions were fluid and messy, and my problem-solving, type A, sequential brain seemed to be no match for disorderly emotions. I spent a great deal of time working with Ashley on this. I practically begged her to carve these emotions off of me like my surgeon had done the tumor.

Curiously, it was usually about ten days after chemo when unruly emotions would strike each time. In hindsight, I wonder if this sadness materialized from a cellular level, courtesy of Cytoxin and Taxotere messing with the hippocampus in my brain. Regardless, emotions laced their tendrils and tightened their grip around me as I navigated my way through grief.

After chemo number one, I thought of my challenge in its entirety, and when I thought of the reality of what I was fighting for, when thoughts of my own mortality took center stage, the fear of me not being enough to beat it took hold. *I could die. What if I die? What if I fought hard, but lost?* I had big plans to make it till I was 95, and I would do everything in my power to make that happen. I wanted to be the crazy old lady doing the hokey-pokey on her birthday. I wanted to shake my cane at people just for comedic relief.

Whenever I was faced with a challenge in life, a goal of some kind, I pushed hard. I was furious with myself if I ever fell short. *I couldn't fall short here! I could die!* What if I really wasn't strong enough, or brave enough, or just enough? I knew it was okay to be sad and feel defeated. *But what did it mean if I became defeated in this story?* That thought haunted me.

I didn't want to die. I didn't want to leave my babies. It was my job as their mother to protect them, to love them, to be there for them. There were so many milestones I just didn't want to miss. One night, when I tucked my children in bed and kissed them gently on the foreheads, I looked over them and smiled. I thought to myself: *I'd shave my hair every day for the rest of my life if it meant that I could stay here with them, be here with them, hold them, love them, hug them…every single day.* Bargaining.

With the loss of my breasts, my hair, and my health, part of who I was had died. I would never be that same person again. It felt as if I'd lost part of my identity, and it was a tragic, trauma-inducing loss. Sadness soon became this overflowing, unmanageable beast that was drowning me. While I was busy pretending it wasn't there, the power it had over me had grown. It grabbed a hold of me and tugged me under. Depression.

I could feel myself withdrawing from people. I wanted to curl up in a hole somewhere, away from everybody. I became disappointed in myself for being unable to "fix me," physically and emotionally. I felt broken, betrayed by my own body, emotionally gutted, and I had no clue how to tape the pieces back together. I didn't want to be around people; I didn't want to do anything. *Who was this stranger? And how could I get rid of her?*

My shaved hair came out in gobs. Every time I took a shower and ran my hands across my head, fragments of hair would stick to my hands. It was like petting a cat that wouldn't stop shedding. Soon, I had only a few straggly spikes of hair that remained. I was glad that I'd shaved my hair because this was heartbreaking enough. I supposed having it all fall out was at the very least a step towards having this nightmare behind me.

I had an emotional meltdown following chemo number two as well. This time it wasn't just sadness that I was fighting off with a stick, but anger and guilt joined the party too. I was exhausted and frustrated once more. It felt very chemical, completely out of my ability to control. I truly felt battered by these waves; I was tired, I was sick, and I hated it! I had fallen once again; and I was unnecessarily harsh and angry with myself every time I did.

I wanted to be stronger; and I was unkind to myself during these moments…beating myself up for somehow not surviving this better…with more ease…or grace…or anything other than exhaustion and tears. I realize now we must give ourselves credit where credit is due, and some days the best we can do is simply make it through the damn day…breathe…keep breathing.

To my dismay, anger and fear united with sadness, and together, they were powerful and relentless. They drained me of any sense of control over my own being and locked forces while I watched as my body continued to get ripped away from me bit by bit. I needed a way to shake myself from their chokehold; I needed a way to not be suffocated, a way to feel like my body *really* did belong to me.

I later learned that this profound grief just needed to be heard and felt, however terrifying that may have been. No emotion lasts forever; and we are strong enough to feel them. We can't scratch them out of existence, or use a melon-baller to carve, say, fear off of us. Emotions are, by design, part of us. Fear, for example, isn't always the bad guy. Feeling fear is what elevates our cortisol and initiates the 'fight or flight' response in times of danger. Its role is to protect us.

I was still trying to force positivity and optimism to shine through and to shun any negative emotions that sprouted. I wanted nothing to do with them. I tried to push them back, like a sibling taunting you on a long road trip. *You can ride in this car with me, but stay on your side of the line.* I felt these emotions were a nuisance, a handful, and I was about done. What more could I possibly take?

After round three of chemo, I was grateful and optimistic that I had the worst behind me, but I was also just as disheartened with my body when it failed me, and it continued to fail me. Chemo had me confined to my bed; fatigue and bone pain had me crippled and crashing, and I wasn't strong enough to will them away. I was powerless against these drugs, and I hated that my body would not do as I commanded.

Losses continued to pile high as I navigated my way through the deepest waters of grief. There was the loss of control over my body from chemo. There was the obvious physical loss of my breasts; but still, there was a trickling effect of what all that continued to cost me. My expanders were hard and painful. I couldn't lie on my stomach or have pressure put on my chest from so much as an embrace without there being intense pain. My body physically hurt for my husband to hug me or for my children to lean on me at bedtime stories. I'd even lost the sensation of my own touch. It was as if I was disappearing: first physically and then emotionally.

Though I would eventually have implants and come to love and honor the new me, I had to first grieve for the memory of a body I no longer owned. My body was not mine and my heart ached for its loss. My ovaries had to go too; it was no longer safe for me to keep them. *It's not safe for me to keep a body part that I've owned my entire life?* I couldn't win. There was no reprieve. *How was I to breathe? How was I to stand? How could I possibly plan for all that I didn't know?* I guess that was kind of the point: I couldn't. This did not digest well for me—the over-planner and control freak.

I had come to know emptiness and grief, and like *Harry Potter and the Order of the Phoenix*, I felt as if I too had seen my first Thestral (Rowling 2003). Part of who I was had died— the person I had been my entire life, and that was tragic and frightening.

On the same token, despite all that I had been cheated out of, I had been gifted an extraordinary perspective. To credit this great tribulation with the creation of acceptance and courage was indeed ironic and a work in progress. After all, I suppose it was true what my therapist had said time and again: "We are all constant works in progress, and that is okay."

Through this darkness, I came to know compassion: compassion others had shown for me, as well as compassion I had towards them. Empathy grew, as well as gratitude and vulnerability. What beautiful hues of color this darkness could bring! I could appreciate and understand the hardships others faced. This newer level of compassion could allow me to show up for people in ways I might not have previously known.

Through my anguish, I somehow summoned fortitude. I was not always the greatest at recognizing this or giving myself credit, but there were other moments when I did indeed feel the presence of incredible strength. I was strong. I was resilient. I would survive. I would pick myself up, dust myself off, and find the Neosporin (whatever form it took in the moment of pain). I'd break out of my caged chrysalis soon enough.

Token of Courage: Feel all the Feels

Grief is an undeniable part of this process. You may find yourself bouncing from Denial to Bargaining to Depression to Anger and back to Denial again. You may even feel that you have arrived to Acceptance, only to find yourself back in Denial once more. We may not be able to control our emotions, but we can choose how we handle them. We can allow ourselves to feel them and recognize what they are without judging them. No emotion will last forever; emotions are like waves, they rage and recede.

Courage Token #11: Feel all the feels.

Chapter 12

Broken and Bright

Nugget of Knowledge

Marsha Linehan, the founder of DBT, says, "Radical acceptance rests on letting go of the illusion of control and a willingness to notice and accept things as they are right now, without judging" (2019). Linehan explains that rejecting our realities doesn't change them, rather it leads to suffering. Although acceptance may cause a period of sadness, Linehan has observed that "deep calmness usually follows."

To radically accept an experience or emotion doesn't mean that you have to agree with it. It's more about acknowledging its existence: *I see you; I feel you; I acknowledge your presence without judgement and without it defining me.*

It makes me smile to think of Grand Master Oogway, the turtle from *Kung Fu Panda*, when he talks to Shifu about Tai Lung's escape. Shifu runs up in a panic saying that he has bad news, but Master Ooway calmly responds, "Aah, Shifu. There's just news. There's no good or bad." I'd say that this turtle is practicing some radical acceptance here. But then, when Master Oogway hears that Tai Lung actually escaped and was on his way to the village, there's a bit of comedic relief when Oogway's eyes bulge a bit with trepidation and he freezes for a second, finally saying, "That is bad news" (Stevenson and Osborne 2008). I chuckle every time I think of that scene; and it brings a sense of calming and acceptance despite Master

Oogway's admittance of bad news. It reminds me that though radical acceptance may be the goal, we may not always be perfectly calm or agreeable with that acceptance, and that's okay too.

Part of radical acceptance is embracing the present moment, sometimes with a practice such as mindfulness. Mindfulness is when you're able to connect with all that you are and where you are in the present moment. It is a skill that requires practice, but can be refined through working with a counselor, through the use of an app, or even through exercises like yoga or Qigong. It's about savoring the present tense: What do you see, hear, feel right now? It grounds you in the here and now rather than letting your mind run wild to all of the what-ifs down the road. It was a great technique to use when going to follow-up appointments and not wanting to get out of the car. My mind would race to either the past (*last time I was here they cut me; my body was hurt*) or the future (*they might find more cancer and then I have to fight it all over again*). Staying mindful in the moment would have me focusing on the current sights, sounds, and smells. Sometimes I'd even repeat the phrase that Ashley had told me, "I may be in the same place, but I am in a different place in time."

Another practice that often helped me was listening to slow soft music while doing yoga, focusing on the breath, and echoing to myself over and over again, "This is *my* body, *my* mind, *my* soul...*my* body, *my* mind, *my* soul." My friend Michelle would even say, "Thank your body. Thank your breath. Thank your heartbeat. Your body has *not* betrayed you; rather, it is still there carrying you day in and day out despite everything else."

Personal Voyage

My brother and I, along with my friend Beth, were the three musketeers growing up. We had a lot of fun and got into a lot of trouble too. We made countless forts, climbed trees, invented our own games, and played *Top Gun* while riding our bikes at mach speed. We made brains for a haunted house by squeezing tubes of toothpaste into a bowl. We played a game called 'Mud Queen', which always got us into trouble. It involved us jumping from pillow to pillow, sliding, squealing, and avoiding the carpet (or 'mud') at all costs. We were eventually told not to play that game anymore; however, we were great at being kids and didn't always listen! We experimented, explored, pushed our limits, and usually learned something along the way.

One day when our mothers went for a walk, we decided that a pillow fight was a great idea. We tossed giant throw pillows through the air and targeted one another as if we were having a snowball fight. Unfortunately, one of these massive 'snowballs' sailed into my mother's antique porcelain lamp—one that my grandfather (who died when my mom was five) had bought for my grandmother. It was inevitably caught by the tiled floor and shattered into pieces. HOLY SHIT! She was surely going to kill us; what were we going to do in the few moments that we had left to live?

The genius engineers that we were decided that *we* could put the lamp back together, and she would be none the wiser. So, naturally, we grabbed the scotch tape and set off to assemble the shattered lamp. With our trusty elementary school adhesive in hand and our 3D puzzle solving skills, how could we possibly fail?

Yep, we failed.

Scotch tape was not strong enough to hold porcelain together, and the lamp wobbled and sagged under the tape's lame attempt to piece it back together.

We executed plan B, adding our second most trusted elementary school aged adhesive to the mix: Elmer's glue. Needless to say, it did not help our cause. The lamp was soon covered in globs of white sticky glue and tape. It did not stand eloquently on its own, rather it danced and wobbled and sagged once more. When our mothers returned and saw our ingenuity and the shattered heirloom, we begged them to yell at us. However, my mom didn't say a word. Her silence was more punishment than we could have ever thought possible; we felt horrible.

I have thought of this lamp often. It eventually became a funny tale from our youth; but more recently, I was reminded of it while trying to piece my life back together. I felt like that broken lamp; I was in the scotch tape and Elmer's glue stage of my journey. I looked for adhesives, for purpose and acceptance of myself. I gathered up the pieces of my brokenness, studied them, tried to make meaning of them. I might have wobbled while trying to stand; I may have collapsed and failed a time or two, but I would shine my light in a room again. I didn't know how I'd get put back together; I just believed that I would.

Eventually, my mom's lamp was put back together. I don't know how it came to be whole again, but it did. If you look closely at the lamp now, you can still see the cracks from where it was busted apart. Nonetheless, it was made whole once more. It was able to stand on its own and shine its light in a room.

One of my friends wrote me the sweetest letter where she voiced that I was a rock to so many, that I was strong and was facing cancer with grace and optimism; that I didn't let cancer stop me from living. How was *this* version of myself so difficult for me to see? All I felt was the weight of the porcelain, the unpleasant stickiness of glue and tape, and the deep cracks that broke my being; yet she saw the light from the lamp.

* * *

Bryan had arranged for me to do a photoshoot before, during, and after my own storm. I was discovering a new me, and it was getting captured both in photo and in print. In the beginning, I summoned strength. I numbed and shielded myself with optimism and humor. I was modest in revealing both my physical and emotional identity. The ironic thing was, as I continued to move through the treatment and recovery, I realized that optimism was only a shield to hide behind. True strength and happiness resided with radical acceptance of my full self.

Michelle encouraged me to showcase this truth: the truth of my scars and the truth of my identity. I braved a newer understanding of myself. Mackensey (my photographer) and I spoke a lot about how vulnerability, love for ourselves, strength, and courage were inseparable. She captured the truth of not only my scars and the pain that I had endured, but also the truth of my emotional identity. I had strength not because I leaned solely on optimism and humor, but rather because I had experienced

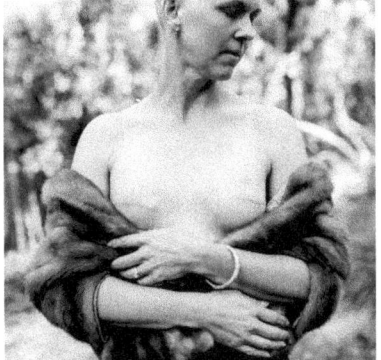

Fig. 18. Joyce "During the Storm" photoshoot in October 2017 at Wormsloe Historic Site in Savannah, GA.
Photograph by Mackensey Alexander.

121

it all. I was strong and rose each time because I laughed and cried, because I had faced fear and gratitude, and because I had sought the light from love and compassion within. Mackensey told me that when dandelions got cut down, they grew back twice as strong. I wanted to be a dandelion.

I know of older women, survivors, who during their time of need felt immense shame for having to undergo a mastectomy in the first place. Admitting to the world that they had to lose part of what defined their womanhood was somehow a taboo topic. The very word *mastectomy* seemed shameful and inappropriate for discussion.

Thank goodness our society has grown in knowledge and compassion, and speaking these once forbidden words is no longer shameful. The women who came before me are my heroes. They paved the way so that when cancer came knocking on my own door, I wasn't afraid to speak about it. I was able to actually say, "*I had a mastectomy,*" without shame. I didn't have to stuff it away in some box and pretend that it wasn't a part of me. Shame still came for me but it manifested a bit differently than for those generations back.

I set out on a mission to pave the way for the generations after me. I wanted to advocate for others, let them know that they weren't alone. I wanted to dismantle this shame even more for the generations that would follow me. I set out to do that by sharing my story—sharing my pain and how I found the courage to rise again.

Mackensey, my photographer, captured much of this during the Goddess Sessions, especially the *During the Storm* collection. In a single photograph, she captured a critical message that I wanted all women to hear. She captured the true heartache and grief that accompanied my maimed body, while simultaneously capturing a sense of peace and inner beauty. One photograph seemed to shout: *We hurt and we bleed, but we are courageous, and we will rise again.*

This message was meant to be shouted at the tops of mountains; this was something that shouldn't be hidden from the world. We are not victims of a heartless disease; rather, we are warriors…wounded but not defeated. We are women who have braved the unthinkable

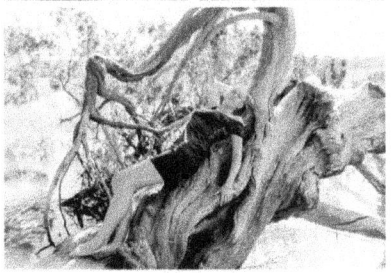

Fig. 19. Photo of Joyce "During the Storm."
Photograph by Mackensey Alexander.

and are stronger because of it. We are your mothers, your daughters, your wives, and your friends; and together we rise and weather this storm!

However, when I was asked if this powerful photo could be shared to help other women, I froze. It was my own shame rearing its head! I was torn. I had chunks of my body carved off of me, foreign objects embedded and sewn beneath my skin, and muscles stretched to allow for reconstruction. I had endured poisons pumped into my heart and streamed throughout my system. I had to watch as my hair follicles died and let go of the strands that they once held.

You see, the question crossed my mind: *Would I want my friends/family—or strangers— to see that? What about my children? Their friends? How could this be used against me? Against them?* There it was…a petri dish for shame, and it grew. I wanted to cower and hide my scars. I wanted to hide who I was and what I'd been through all over again. I was fearful that someone would see my scars and judge or shun or ridicule me in some way. *How dare they!* I was trying to play out scenes in my head and predict people's responses in efforts to somehow control the message I wanted to send out into the world. I wanted to ensure people would hear what I was actually saying and avoid any misconceptions that could breed more shame.

After wrestling it out, I decided it was worth the risk of sharing. I knew I couldn't control people's perceptions or responses, and I wanted to make sure everyone knew it was possible to move past their own scars, whatever they were. I heard Keala Settle (2017) singing "This is Me" from The Greatest Showman in my head:

I won't let them break me down to dust. I know that there's a place for us. For we are glorious…I am brave, I am bruised, I am who I'm meant to be, this is me…Look out 'cause here I come and I'm marching on to the beat I drum. I'm not scared to be seen. I make no apologies. This is me.

It was radical acceptance of my body—of myself—that gave me the courage to share my message. Fighting my new reality and hiding my body and my story in shame was not going to change what had already happened. Putting myself out there sent the message that there was nothing to be ashamed of. In fact, there was something to be proud of.

Token of Courage: Learn to Embrace

It's easy to criticize and compare, to fixate on what we've lost, to be stuck in the past or in denial, or to yearn for what we lack. It's easy to assign a judgment of "good" or "bad" on things about ourselves, about our bodies, on experiences we have, and situations we are in. But the truth is, sometimes things just are. Applying value judgments to everything does not change what already is, and it can exacerbate and prolong suffering. The more you fight reality and refuse to accept, the more pain you create. Even still, acceptance does not mean you have to like it.

I had the choice to deem the changes to my body as shameful or to see the beauty in the scars that proved my strength. This body is my boat, the vehicle that affords me life. It is mine, and it is who I am—down to the stitches that have sewn me together, like the pieces of the broken lamp. It is beautiful that no matter the shape, no matter the size, no matter the losses or the scars, my body is still here, still breathing, still carrying me day after day and year after year.

For token of courage #12, embrace. I challenge you to radically accept yourself as you are, without making any judgements. Embrace your own bodies, your own scars. Embrace the brokenness. Whatever your reality may be right now, try to embrace rather than resist. Breathe and be here. Your body is the vessel that carries you through life; and that in and of itself makes it one of the most coveted and beautiful things in the world. So, take care of it; protect it; love it; and do not apologize for any piece of it.

Chapter 13

The Power of Vulnerability

Nugget of Knowledge

In her book *Daring Greatly,* Brené Brown teaches that connection, love, and happiness stem from vulnerability. She talks about how everyone has shame and that when we experience it, we should practice authenticity with each other. Empathy, according to Brené, is the antidote to shame, and to move from shame to empathy requires connection (Brown 2012). True connection is formed when we are vulnerable with one another.

When we speak our truth out loud in a safe, compassionate environment, it can truly heal us. Every single one of us is broken because we are human. As my friend, Jenny, puts it, "We all speak from our own scars, whatever they may be."

The process of unmasking our emotional truth and creating connections with those having similar experiences requires us to be vulnerable. Some examples of vulnerability might be: taking chances that might lead to someone rejecting you, talking about your weaknesses or perceived failures, being honest about what you need in a relationship, or sharing information publicly that you might normally keep to yourself. All of these examples require risk, but the reward is feeling less isolated and alone. It also helps us to grow as individuals. According to psychiatrist Dr. Daniel B. Block, "The inability or unwillingness to be vulnerable in important relationships creates a limit on how much those relationships can evolve and deepen. Not being vulnerable hampers the development of intimacy in relationships" (Fritscher 2023).

The caveat to vulnerability is that not all environments are safe for deep personal sharing. It is wise to practice discernment when taking risks toward deeper intimacy, ensuring that a reasonable amount of safety and trust are present. However, at the end of the day, it is always a leap of faith to reveal your true feelings to another person or group, and the risk is almost always worth the reward.

Personal Voyage

I gave a presentation on "Survivor Truths" to a group of cancer peers. I'd given it before and been greeted with countless confirmations. Connection had been created; survivors were given permission to be human, to learn how to cope with their emotions, and to push forward and live their best lives possible despite their pain. More importantly, they were able to recognize that they weren't alone. It was a great moment, and it renewed me with purpose and conviction.

However, at this particular presentation, when I was sharing about fear, a woman in the group commented that she did not relate with what I was saying at all. Truthfully, I was dumbfounded. This was the first I had ever heard of this. *A cancer warrior void of fear?* I wondered if what I had said might have jabbed a little too closely to a wound she was fiercely guarding. It was as if fear was the enemy and by extension I was perceived as a threat. She told me she didn't have room for fear because she was deeply religious and "where there was fear there was no God." She told me that fear and faith could not coexist; and then she asked me pointedly, "Do you even believe in God?" *Sting*. My vulnerability went crashing to the floor, and shame for admitting my truths about fear began to rise.

My inner critic was loud on the drive home. It felt like there were a hundred fingers pointed at me, declaring my faith less than real if I was caught fraternizing with fear. *I do believe in God. I do have faith. I have faith; and I have fear. Joyce, you admitted that you have fear, ergo you must not have faith.* More tears. More shame. More reason for me to hush my true emotions and deny their existence at all. *That can't be right. Can it?*

Since I haven't studied theology, and I know that I'm not even close to being a qualified professional at interpreting scripture, I did the best that I could. I first turned to Google to search for scriptures about fear. Here's what I found:

1 John 4:18 "There is no fear in love. But perfect love drives out fear because fear has to do with punishment. The one who fears is not made perfect in love."

1 Corinthians 16:13: "Be on your guard; stand firm in faith; be courageous; be strong."

Psalm 18:2 "The LORD is my rock, my fortress, and my deliverer."

Isaiah 41:10 "So do not fear, for I am with you; do not be dismayed, for I am your God. I will strengthen you and help you; I will uphold you in my righteous right hand."

Micah 7:8 "Though I have fallen, I will arise; though I sit in darkness, the LORD will be my light."

I hear faith. I hear love. I hear a Father calming His children. I hear that I am not perfect, but He is still my rock. *What am I missing?* All I knew was that I was hurting and confused. I picked up the phone and called my scripture-quoting, cancer-fighting friend who had wrestled with her own humanity countless times before. I knew she was a safe person to call; she would give me her honest perspective without offense or judgement. It's funny how God brings people and situations into your life at just the right moment in time.

She told me it was not a coincidence that I was asking; she had wrestled with that very sentiment when someone had told her, "Faith and fear cannot coexist." However, a friend reminded her they can coexist. "That's the nature of being human. We are not God. We are not perfect."

Furthermore, fear is a requirement for keeping us safe. Our emotions, even if they are negative and unpleasant, are not out to hurt us. Biologically speaking, fear is a vital emotion to our survival. It notifies us when things are dangerous and stimulates a response…all in efforts to keep us safe. In *What Part of the Brain Controls Emotions,* Seladi-Schulman explains that in regards to fear, the amygdala stimulates the hypothalamus signaling adrenal glands to produce adrenaline and cortisol, thus activating the fight or flight response (Seladi-Schulman 2018). All of our emotions play a critical role in our lives. They tell us about something and initiate a response that gets communicated to those nearest us.

The 'fight or flight' response that accompanies fear shaking the reins in the amygdala of our brains…it has served us well over the years. Fear gives us what we need in times of great danger. Do we fight the wild animal or do we run and hide? We don't go up to it and say, "Hey what's up!" Do I shield my face when a ball comes hurling at it, or do I try to catch it? We don't stand there and wait for it to hit.

It's understandable then, that when my brain gets the message: *I've been here before. There's danger inside this building. They told you that you had cancer here. There are knives in there, sharp ones that were used to cut off parts of your body. Danger!* That fear is trying to protect me. It shouldn't be shunned or shamed for that noble job. Perhaps it needs to be calmed and reassured but not removed from my being entirely. It is that same fear—fear of the cancer itself—that motivates me to go to my check-ups.

When I was told, "Where there is fear, there is no God," I felt like my own worthiness had been called into question. Shame for feeling fear and then again for admitting it rose up high in my heart, and vulnerability went rolling off my sleeve and thudded onto the ground. But through my unpleasant thud, I was connected with another and compassion did bloom.

The woman who brought this concept to my attention during my presentation was not wrong. She was managing and fiercely protecting her own wounds in the best way that she knew how. Perhaps that was her mantra. Perhaps those words were her life preserver, and who was I to puncture that? She had lived through her own stormy waters, had to deal with things no woman should and had her own story to tell.

And speaking of stories, I had more work of my own to do. Sharing my own story in a raw and completely unpolished way was an important step in the journey of braving the newer version of myself. Bryan told me there was power in vulnerability; in letting others see all of you and not trying to hide any piece of who you are. The light that exists within us all is fueled with raw honesty and love for who we are. Only then can it radiate outward, encourage others to do the same, and let empathy take root. So, I decided to post the raw honest truth online. I aimed to showcase my journey in its entirety.

For the first time, I admitted to the world that I didn't always have it together, that I had been going to see a therapist. It was out there. Every part of me was there for the world to read. I'm not going to lie; it was empowering. It was freeing and inspiring to be reminded that we were all going through something and none of us were flying through it flawlessly.

Token of Courage: Share Your Story

My post shared publicly:

My husband told me there was power in showing your vulnerability, because it meant that you were comfortable being and feeling however you were rather than how others might expect you to be. Since I am beginning to care less about what people think of me right now (perhaps cancer is the catalyst in changing me in more ways than one), here's the real me: authentic, sincere, and vulnerable.

I am an optimist; I like to smile and laugh. I'm compassionate, sympathetic, outgoing; I'm a freaking damn delight! I color coordinate my planner because it makes sense, and it's awesome. I plan, organize, and coordinate just about anything: parties, trips, school...the list is endless. (Y'all know you love me for it). I arrive early for everything, because being early is on-time, and on-time is late.

I'm a perfectionist. I'm a people pleaser. I care way too much about way too many things. Worrying has been an art form, a talent of mine since the beginning. Former teachers of mine will shake their heads and smile because they have witnessed this. They know. My friends know. This is me. I want my life to be in this nice, neatly packaged bundle complete with a shiny bow.

So, what happens when life gets messy and I don't know how to clean it up? Here's another layer of vulnerability: I've gone to see a therapist. I've been a handful of times now, long enough for her to get me; and now that I'm up against some pretty ugly messes in my life, it's been helpful. I guess most of us don't want to admit that asking for help could prove beneficial in ways we never thought; I was no different. There seems to be this fear that people will think something is wrong with you. (But, y'all already know that I'm a damn delight.)

We all have layers to our personality and sides that we try to hide from the world. I am no different. I don't want anyone to know when my smile fades or when I feel defeated. But here it is: Cancer is trying to kill me, and that, folks, is not just messy, it's kind of fucking sad. My smile does fade at that thought.

Most of the time I am hopeful and strong, but I am human and have tough days too. I'm learning that grief born from adversity isn't something you can push through and find yourself unscathed on the other side. There is a piece of who I once was, both physically and emotionally, that has died in some ways. I will never again be the person I was prior to my diagnosis. I am forever changed.

I have scars: physical and emotional, and although they may fade over time, they have left their marks upon me. I'm not saying that's a bad thing either. I'm merely recognizing that when something in your life rocks your foundation, and the ground you have relied on for years slips like a rug ripped from underneath you, the change you experience in yourself is accelerated and intensified. I have to let myself be happy when I am happy, sad when I am sad, and somehow learn to not judge myself for that.

I will make it through this darkness. I don't know how, or when, or who I will be at that moment in time. However, I have hope. In the beginning, when I stood at the entrance to this dark forest, I thought I could leave a trail of breadcrumbs for those behind me. I wanted to light the way for my girls and anyone else who may be traveling this spooky path and clutching their fear along the way. I wanted to make it better for them, or at least easier.

Unfortunately, I am also learning that there is no one way out! I can't show them the way, because there are so many routes, and they are as individual as the people taking them. The path you take in life is yours. It's your story, and nobody can write it for you. There is, however, a difference between walking your own way and walking alone. You may have to be the one to walk, but this doesn't mean you are without support.

Cancer really is changing me. Although my transformation is yet to be completed (I still have a heavy fight to withstand), I can feel this new sense of boldness trying to rise. I want to let it rise.

There's a lull in time now, a pause between one cause for action and the next. This is the time when my body and mind collapse. It's when everything I haven't had time to face creeps up and must be processed. I'm not going to lie; it's no picnic. I don't want to be sad. I like my smile. Although, to be fair to myself, it's a bit unrealistic to expect myself to never experience sadness when cancer is trying to kill me. I will fight it, and I will find joy again.

I will harness my determination, hope, and positivity and get through this, but that doesn't mean I should be afraid of grief, of being sad. It's going to be there too. I don't want to ignore it and let it grow uncontrollably in the shadows, nor do I wish to adopt it as a new motto.

Yet, in the movie "Inside Out," Joy even let Sadness take control of core memories (Docter, 2015). By the end of the movie, they had these beautiful marbled memories infused with multiple hues of emotions. Some were a mix of anger and disgust, some of joy and sadness. I have found myself with moments of such intertwined emotions: gratitude and anger, happiness and sorrow; although opposites, they were sometimes inseparable and felt at the same moment in time. I guess my best advice for my children, for others struggling, and for myself as well is to let yourself be whoever you are in that moment and don't feel bad about it.

Chapter 14

Light the Night with Hope

Nugget of Knowledge

One out of eight women are diagnosed with breast cancer, and early detection is absolutely critical for one's survival. According to *Survival Rates for Breast Cancer,* written by the American Cancer Society (2020), the five-year survival rates for breast cancer based on women diagnosed with *localized* breast cancer was as high as 99%. The same article shows that if breast cancer is *regional* (it may have spread to nearby lymph nodes, but has no evidence of having metastasized), then the five-year survival rate is still relatively high, 86%. However, if the breast cancer is *distant* (already metastasized to lungs, liver, or bones), then the five-year survival rate drops to 27%.

Of course, these numbers are not absolutes; there are other variables to consider when determining your personal prognosis, so please have this personal discussion with your provider. However, it is clear that there is something to be said for early detection, for finding your cancer before it has had the chance to spread. So, be proactive with your surveillance.

In addition to having your annual screening mammogram done (and/or calling the doctor if you notice anything out of the norm for you and your body), women should do monthly self-breast exams. Early detection is critical; the five-year survival rate hinges greatly on whether or not it has metastasized. So, be familiar with your own body; or, as one survivor put it, "Know your own geography."

Personal Voyage

During the lull in time between chemo and my hysterectomy, I worked on piecing myself together emotionally as well as processing all I had previously braved and still had yet to face. You could see in my eyes and my wounds I had been physically and emotionally tormented. Processing fear like I had never known before was exhausting and relentless. I imagined what kind of Christmas my girls would have without their mother. *What would Bryan do? Would my family know how much I love them?* Perhaps this was the planner in me: trying to make sure we were all prepared.

Fig. 20. Photo of Joyce "During the Storm."
Photograph by Mackensey Alexander.

I wrote my kids a letter to read should I die. It was the hardest thing that I have ever written, mostly because I feared that I was actually going to die. How do you wrap up in words your love, capture memories of you with your kids, try to assure them that everything will be okay, let them know that you want the best for them in life, that you believe in them, that you would do anything for them, and yet say goodbye while feeling like you're going to miss all of this? How do you prepare for that?

Post-hysterectomy I knew I would wake up from anesthesia with an instantaneous loss of estrogen. If chemo contributed to the intensity of negative emotions on a cellular level, then what would happen to me when my ovaries were removed and the chemistry within my body changed drastically overnight and for good? Could it plunge me into a pit deeper than the ones I had previously known? One survivor I spoke with was all too familiar with this darkness. She told me, "Joyce, these are not pits; they are tunnels."

My nerves were frazzled and worn thin as my surgery date approached. Over Thanksgiving, I developed a bit of a cough. I wanted to take Nyquil, but I read that I should avoid it prior to surgery since it could increase the risk of bleeding. I also discovered that the combination of a cough and anesthesia could increase my risk for aspiration during surgery. I resorted to an old-fashioned remedy: mixed one tablespoon of honey with one teaspoon of lemon juice and one teaspoon of whiskey; and hoped for the best. Thankfully, my cough disappeared just in time for surgery.

Soon, I received a call regarding directions for the day prior to surgery. That evening, I was to take a Fleet enema and then chug two Gatorades at midnight. *What the hell was happening?* I had cancer, had endured countless procedures, was mustering up the courage to have organs slashed out of me, and here I was being told for shits and giggles that an enema was required too. My life was at its peak!

I tucked my children in bed, and it took all of my strength not to break down in tears. I was terrified of surgery. I had hope and faith that all would work out as it should, but I was afraid of what that meant. *Was I kissing my children for the last time?*

I went to bed at 10 p.m., woke up at midnight to chug the two damn Gatorades and then woke up for real at 3:15 a.m. We were supposed to be at the hospital to check in at 5 a.m. Staying true to my "early is on time" motto, we arrived 30 minutes early. We were so early that the hospital doors were still locked.

Once we were inside, we sat down with our overnight bags and tried to relax as the sweet aroma of morning coffee perfumed the air. It was a cruel scent for the fasting coffee lover who craved just a bit of morning comfort. The news played in the background on the overhead TV, and the weatherman spoke of an approaching southern snow storm. *Snow in Coastal Georgia?* I tried to calm myself, take deep breaths, and shake the nerves that rattled within me. I snuggled under the warm coat draped across my shoulders and leaned up against Bryan. He kissed me and told me he loved me.

A nurse soon called my name. I acknowledged my identity and shuffled through the halls to my destination. I was barely awake, cold, and attempted small talk in efforts to sweep my growing anxieties away. As we rounded the second corridor, she pointed to my room.

I was given compression hose, socks, and a gown. I had to literally fight with the hose. It was like trying to stuff your entire leg into an infant's unstretchable sock—it's not fucking possible. Magic was the only explanation I had for how those damn things ever got on. I followed the rest of the preparatory instructions and climbed into the gurney.

I told the nurse about my anxiety and my detailed memory from the previous operating room. She was shocked that I had remembered all that I had and told me not to worry, that she would give me half of the "I don't give a shit cocktail" now, and the second half right before they wheeled me back.

The doctors made their morning rounds to see me prior to

surgery. I remembered seeing the anesthesiologist and telling him about my family's hemorrhaging history; he was reassuring and told me not to worry. Shortly afterwards, the nurse gave me the first half of my cocktail. It hit me fast, and I barely remember speaking with Dr. Pearl. He said he would be doing his portion of the surgery first, and he was ready whenever we were.

The OR nurse came to wheel me back. I felt my nerves starting to rise, but I must have gotten my second dose of cocktails right around then because my memories become very fuzzy about being wheeled back this time. I don't remember getting on the table, only them fastening my "seatbelt" and someone asking if that size belt was too big for me. The only other thing I remember was them putting a mask over my face, telling me to breathe; and then I was out.

The next thing I remember was a woman standing over me, shouting my name frantically, "Joyce? Joyce, wake up! Wake up, Joyce!" Bright lights beamed overhead, and I didn't want to wake up. *Leave me alone, and let me roll over.* They kept shaking and shouting at me until I acknowledged them. Accompanying my developing lucidness was also a growing sense of pain. *Ouch!* I hurt. I hurt badly.

They told me the nurse would have pain meds in my room, so they worked towards swiftly wheeling me in that direction. I wanted to hurry up and get there so that my growing awareness of pain could be managed. When we finally reached my room, I had the I-have-to-pee sensation. Normally, I was self-conscious and tried to do everything on my own; but I was groggy, in pain, and I didn't care who saw what. They helped me shuffle to the restroom, where I tried to relieve the sensation, but couldn't actually go. The motion of standing and walking immediately made me feel sick. They told me I couldn't have any pain meds while I felt queasy for concern of throwing them right back up. *Wait, what? I couldn't get anything to alleviate my pain?* I wanted to cry.

They encouraged me to order lunch and eat something; they could give me medicine once I could keep food down. Thankfully, they ordered me a one-dose shot of morphine to cut the pain and allow me the chance to focus on food. Bryan came to my room around this time and helped me order lunch. Surgery had commenced at 7:30 a.m. and I was wheeled into my room around 10:30 a.m. I remember passing in and out of sleep, and the only food I remember eating was chocolate pudding.

Once I was discharged, Bryan pulled the car up to the circle out in front of Day Surgery while the nurse loaded me up and wheeled me out to the curb in a wheelchair. It was freezing outside, so I shuffled to the car, padded myself with pillows, and turned up the heat. We were on our way home.

Left foot, right foot, and so the pattern went. I inched my way through recovery once more, trying to soak up the holiday spirit surrounding me. The lights on the Christmas tree were warm and bright; the colorfully wrapped presents topped with homemade bows made my heart happy. However, when I saw the reflection of my naked body, I fought the urge to fall to the floor in grief. I was maimed; it looked like I had survived the brutalities of war. I had six scars. Upon my chest was the scar from where my port laid beneath it; and then just south of that, were two giant incisions that draped across the curvatures of my newly grown breasts. Although I had become accustomed to seeing these marks, there was something unsettling about recognizing they had been reopened and sewn together once more.

As my eyes drifted southward, they noticed three more incisions marked with surgical tape. Two were on my abdomen, and one was around my belly button. Stains of blood beneath the tape were all I had to imagine what was concealed beneath. I had to wait and let healing occur before I could unmask them and know for certain how disfigured my body had become.

I had developed a bit of postnasal drip and was unable to suffocate the coughing it instigated. Coughing with abdominal stitches was incredibly painful (although sneezing was worse). I squeezed a pillow, pressed it tightly against my stomach and clenched when the coughing ensued. With each uncontrollable outburst of air, it felt like my organs were going to shoot out through my stitches.

Since my ovaries had been removed, my body began to enter a rapid onset of surgically induced menopause. In addition to the fresh physical wounds, the inevitable hot flashes, night sweats, and chills commenced. I knew menopause would cause hot flashes, but I had no idea that they would be followed by chills. Covers were on, and then covers were off. Hats were on, and then hats were off. The thermostat would get turned up, and then it would get turned down.

I still had tape concealing my abdominal wounds when I noticed a red bubble just above my navel at one of the incisions. It was the size of my pinky nail and itched a bit. *Could it be infected?* I called the number provided and spoke with a doctor on call. She had me remove the tape to get a better look at what was going on. This was the first time that I got to see my newly earned scars. The two on the sides were surprisingly small, so

I convinced myself that with some time they would fade away. My belly button had been reconstructed. Although, it didn't look ghastly, it wasn't mine and I knew it.

Moreover, the giant red bubble begged for attention. After explaining what it looked like to the doctor over the phone, she told me that she didn't think that it was an emergency, but she wanted me to follow-up with my surgeon first thing in the morning. When I saw the PA, she wasn't too worried about my spot. Before leaving, I asked if they had my biopsy results back. I'm so glad I asked because she said, "Yes ma'am, they were all benign."

"So, does this mean I am cancer free?" I asked eagerly.

She paused and then confirmed, "Yes. Yes, it does."

I had trudged through the valleys of hell to get to this one moment, this juncture in my journey, and it was a crucial moment in my life. Those words were beautiful, and they were mine to keep. *I made it!* It took a moment for this to seep in.

As I walked the corridors with my mom to the edge of the building, I told her the great news. "I got my biopsy results. I'm cancer free." She gave me a huge hug, smiled, and had tears well in her eyes. Her baby girl had fought and won. I could only imagine what this would be like for a mom. Her little girl got to live. It was the best Christmas present either of us could have ever hoped for.

* * *

Prior to my surgery, my neighbor called one day and said he wanted to talk to me about our neighborhood's annual holiday fundraiser: Light the Night Parade. Every year people would decorate their golf carts with holiday lights and join in a parade that navigated through the streets of our community. There was a bake sale, contests, a band, and Santa and Mrs. Claus usually made an appearance. The proceeds from the event were always donated to a neighbor in our community that was experiencing an intense hardship of one kind or another.

My neighbor asked if this year they could share my story. I was floored. *Why me?* I was truly touched. *Yes*, I thought. *Spread the news of it to anyone that would hear it because early detection was absolutely essential; it saved my life.* Through genetic testing, I discovered that I had the BRCA2 mutation; it was a complete shock since there was no known family history of breast or ovarian cancer. Doctors even told me that if I'd waited until I was 40, my cancer would have spread and killed me.

Awareness breeds action, and if my story could be used to save another life, then shout it from the rooftops. It would be worth it a thousand times over if even one life wouldn't be taken from their families…one mother didn't have to leave her children too young…one teacher, doctor, friend wouldn't be stripped away from leaving their fingerprints in the world and bettering the lives of those they encountered. One life could save countless more in ways we may never have imagined.

When the neighborhood united to work towards moving mountains on my behalf, I vowed to honor that kindness. I aimed to take my struggles and sculpt goodness from them; I didn't want my story to end with me. I wanted other women to hear those beautiful words that I once heard my surgeon say, "Treatable and curable."

My surgery had been on Thursday December 7, 2017. I came home from the hospital on Friday the 8th, and the parade was

Saturday December 9th. Two days after surgery, Bryan carried the family room rocking chair out onto the front porch for me to sit and watch the parade. He loaded me up with jackets and blankets to keep warm, and my mom took the girls to the edge of the driveway to catch candy that was thrown. Seeing my neighbors wave and smile from their decorated golf carts was heartwarming.

Three days after surgery, on December 10, 2017, the doorbell rang. A train of neighborhood children had accompanied their parents; and when I opened the door, the children shouted, "Merry Christmas!" They handed me a holiday box with that year's proceeds nestled inside. It was over $2000. I was overwhelmed with gratitude for the love they had shown me and for the opportunity to save more lives. Bryan, Mom, and I immediately began to brainstorm ways to maximize awareness and the reach of those funds. So, the Monday after surgery, we started contacting local businesses to see if they would be interested in making a donation in conjunction with ours.

When all was said and done, we were able to provide funds for twenty-two other women in our area to receive mammograms. Other women could hear the words, "treatable and curable." I made an appointment with the Executive Director of a breast cancer nonprofit, Aileen, and delivered the proceeds on January 23, 2018.

Mom stayed for about a week after surgery. I was moving and recovering faster than after my mastectomy, but I wasn't able to make the trip North for the holidays as usual. So Mom came back with Dad for Christmas. The excitement and magic in the air was infectious, and I soaked it all in. The girls and their wide eyes full of wonder melted my heart and spread happiness through my veins. I had survived cancer. I got to live. I got to cherish this magic, this love. It was empowering and sobering, and it shook me with meaning.

Mom and Dad helped take the tree and Christmas decorations down before heading back to Virginia, and then Bryan and I began to focus our attention toward the

Fig. 21. Joyce presenting the check on January 23, 2018

new year. Cancer could have 2017; I was moving onward. We welcomed 2018 as a family. I didn't want to go out and be with crowds of people I didn't know; I wanted to look the ones I loved the most in the face, tell them how much I loved them, and toast to a brand new year!

About five weeks after surgery, I had a follow-up appointment with the gynecologic oncologist who had performed the hysterectomy. I'm not sure why I was so nervous; I had already been told that the biopsy was clear and that I was cancer free. Yet, my nerves shook like crazy. One of the residents entered the room with her med student. Tears were hard to shove aside, and I was caught. She smiled at me and told me I was a badass. Everything I

Fig. 22. New Year 2018 Joyce and Sage

was experiencing, she told me, was 100% normal. She asked if I had someone to talk to, and I said yes. *Oh Lord, was I grateful for having entered therapy when I did!*

After my appointment, Bryan walked by my side down the cancer corridor to the beautiful bell. I had won. I had survived. I made it. I grabbed a hold of the string and posed for a picture. *Was I dreaming? Could this really be happening?* Then, I yanked that rope back and forth and heard the most beautiful chime in my life.

Fig. 23. Joyce ringing the cancer free bell

Token of Courage: Foster Hope

The plaque by the bell at the cancer institute reads, "It's tradition that upon completion of therapy you ring this bell loudly to signify to all who hear its sound that HOPE REMAINS! It is a celebration of spirit, a goal reached, and an announcement of a journey that will continue." You see, hope is threaded *throughout* the journey alongside any uncertainty. Hope is not something we obtain at the end of a trial. *Hope isn't at the end; it's along the way.*

When you have moments of clarity and calm, utilize them to relay information to a future you who may be struggling to find hope. You can write yourself a letter, make a video, create a recording, or put together a playlist of songs that say everything you know that you will need to hear. Find a way to get your message in a figurative bottle and throw it into the sea for future-you to find.

When I rang in the New Year with the cancer-free bell, I heard hope. I heard perseverance. I heard love and patience and tears and heartbreak and courage. I heard applause from the other fighters. I heard the smiles and congratulatory words from doctors who work tirelessly at saving people from this disease. I heard the songs from warriors before me: those who survived and those who perished. I heard their hearts and souls singing that the path they blazed was not in vain. I heard the hope from those yet to travel these roads, and I heard their spirits rise with promise. We are not alone; collectively, our stories and our songs would play each time that bell rang. It was the sweetest music I had ever heard.

The melody is contagious and before you know it, the hope matrix flourishes, and the world begins to change. We are all valuable and have the power to make the world a better place. We do it every day. We just don't always see the results; but every single day we push forward with life and, in doing so, set another beautifully crafted domino effect into motion. You help a friend with a flat tire, you teach a child who hates school, you bring dinner to a neighbor, you teach, you advise, you create, you love, you befriend the lonely, you care for the elderly…you are…you do…you live…you change the world. No action is too small.

Whatever battle you face in life, listen to the melodious sound of hope. Don't let fear plunge your head into the sand. Find hope, and let it infiltrate your entire being. Hope has the power to change everything.

Chapter 15

The Bracelet Nobody Wants

Nugget of Knowledge

Unlike chemotherapy, radiation is a localized treatment for cancer. Radiation oncologists target specific areas to treat. Radiation oncologist, Dr. Michael Hasselle, joined me in a *Keepers of the Flame®* podcast, explaining that the current literature supports radiation post-lumpectomy for optimal prognosis, even though not every woman is a candidate for a lumpectomy (Williams 2019, Episode 7). Some women are shocked to hear that following a mastectomy they may be recommended for radiation, too. They often wonder: *Why do I need radiation if they removed all of my breast tissue? What exactly are they radiating?*

In Podcast #7 on radiation therapy, Dr. Hasselle explains there are two contributing factors that weigh heavily on whether or not post-mastectomy radiation is recommended. Although there are other contributing factors, the two biggest factors in post-mastectomy radiation recommendations are: if the tumor size was greater than 5 cm at initial diagnosis, and if there was a macromet of 2 mm or larger in the lymph nodes (Williams 2019, Episode 7).

In general, Dr. Hasselle says that radiation can reduce one's risk of recurrence by three-fold, and it can target lymph nodes that can't be surgically removed. Still, with every medical treatment there are potential side effects; with radiation, you're almost guaranteed to have some kind of skin reaction. Dr Hassselle also explains that modern-day radiation has a much higher energy, which is good because it can penetrate deeper into the body before the full dose is administered. However, with cancers like breast cancer, there is a certain amount of radiation they might want to have treating the skin; so, radiation oncologists might then use a bolus (a tissue equivalent) to bring that dosage back up to the surface (Williams 2019, Episode 7).

Upon initial referral to a radiation oncologist, you first have a consultation. This is when the provider reviews over your specific situation and makes a recommendation. If you are recommended for radiation, the next thing the radiation oncologists do is make a CT map of where they want the radiation to go. They customize the mapping to fit your anatomy because everyone's body cavities are slightly different, the placement of their heart and lungs are not identical, and the target areas may differ from one patient to the next. The radiation oncologist might want to target the chest wall, axillary lymph nodes, all while avoiding other internal organs (Williams 2019, Episode 7).

Radiation treatments occur every day for a handful of weeks depending on your case, and every time they need to ensure you get lined up in the same exact position. The mapping, of course, helps with this; but they also create a mold for you to lay on that conforms to your body. Blue markers (or in some places tattoos) are drawn on you to aid in this precise alignment, and lasers in the room work to ensure correct alignments of the coordinates as well. Dr. Hasselle even explains that modern-day radiation utilizes x-ray pictures prior to each treatment to confirm precision of targeted areas (Williams 2019, Episode 7).

These machines can cost anywhere between two and six

million dollars, and they have several working components. Precision is of the utmost importance; the safety mechanisms will cause the machine to shut down if the slightest thing is off. Dr. Hasselle shared with us that physicists on site work to ensure that the machine's output of radiation dosage has the precision to hit a single point in space within a millimeter of accuracy. To put it into perspective, he shared that it was a full-time job for two employees to service ten machines in the surrounding area. All this being said, if you come in for radiation treatment, and you're unable to have treatment that day due to the machine being down, know that it is because there are these safety measures in place (Williams 2019, Episode 7).

Personal Voyage

I was doing well, riding on the curtails of victory. I was reclaiming my life, and I felt strong! I was running five miles again, revising my book, and shifting my attention towards helping my friends and being present at school functions. My calendar filled up with lunches and get-togethers. I had donated to breast cancer nonprofits, signed up for races, and was getting involved in the community. I attended a nonprofit's grant awards breakfast where they publicly awarded five grantees for the year that supported local programs. I felt honored to witness this moment. It was as if my disease, my pain, somehow played a small part in making this possible.

I still had slight panic attacks when going to see the doctor… *any* doctor. On March 8, 2018 when I pulled into the hospital parking lot for my six-month post mastectomy follow-up with Dr. Rehl (the breast surgeon), I sat in the car…frozen…for a good 15 minutes contemplating my exit strategy. I looked at the doors to the building and cried. I was afraid of hearing the word "again." It felt excruciating! *Just go in there and sign in. Cry, don't cry, who cares? Just get out of the car, and go in there.* I mustered up some courage. Well, truthfully, I had to pee, so it could very well have been too much coffee that broke my paralysis; but regardless, I went in.

Ashley had encouraged me to use grounding in these moments. I closed the car door and inched my way to the hospital doors. I was doing it. I was going to be okay. *Feel that wind, Joyce. Hear that car door? Inhale. See that bird? Exhale. Still feel the earth beneath your feet? Keep walking.*

I entered the exam room where they performed the biopsy back in June. The sights and sounds were accessing a memory I didn't want to pull up. I continued to use grounding until Dr. Rehl entered and greeted me with a smile and a hug. I spoke with her about many of the recent unexpected blessings. She was excited for me and shared in my positivity.

Then she asked if I'd finished radiation.

"No, but I had a mastectomy. I didn't need it. So, I'm done. Right?"

There was a pause.

I'm not sure if I interpreted a microexpression or if fear bubbled up and caused me to blurt out, "Wait. Do I need to call someone and double check? I am done, right?"

Dr. Rehl was calm and thorough; and with my best interests at heart, she said that she wanted to hear from the radiation oncologist directly. So, she put in a call and told me that she'd follow-up with me either way once she heard back from him.

The appointment had gone rather well, I thought. *Way to go, Joyce!* However, there was nothing that could have prepared me for what came next. While driving home and talking with my friend, the phone beeped and I switched over to take the call. It was Dr. Rehl. Bad news hit me once again. The radiation oncologist wanted a consult with me the next morning; he was leaning heavily towards recommending radiation. I was not done after all.

Wait. What? Wasn't this nightmare over? I was done! I held myself together until I hung up the phone, and then I pulled into a gas station and couldn't move. I was in shock. I was plummeting into a pit of hopelessness and grief more intense and powerful than I could have previously imagined. I cried and screamed in the car, gasping for air like I was drowning. My body was shaking, and I was hyperventilating. My breakdown was so intense that strangers came and tapped on my window to see if I was okay. I was not.

I eventually stopped crying enough to start driving home. My friend called me back, and I lost it all over again. I made it home safely, but I could only get one word out every ten breaths or so. I was panicked, horrified, and angry. I felt sick and weak. I leaned on the kitchen table for support.

Finally, my body just collapsed to the floor. I laid on the cold tile of the kitchen floor, curled up in the fetal position. *I can't do this again.* I begged my trusty internal coach for a pep talk. It was as if the great life lessons I'd been learning were truly getting tested. I reasoned that despite this setback, I was still alive! I was still on a journey; and my ending hadn't been written. I echoed my advice in a whisper, soon raising the desperate pep talk to a shout. *Deep breaths! I will rise again.*

Bryan came with me the next morning to meet with the radiation oncologist. I was surprisingly calm and focused after my monumental meltdown the day before. I wanted answers to my long list of questions. Apparently, I was in the gray area. My cancer was 1.2 cm in size, but I had three masses. I wasn't technically lymph node positive because that was defined by the research to be greater than 2 mm in size. Yet, there *was* cancer there. I had what they call a micromet: *one millimeter* of cancerous growth was found in my lymph nodes. This, together with the fact that I had three masses, a genetic mutation, a high-grade tumor, and I was young, made me a candidate for radiation.

I felt like I had just been smacked in the face with a spike-tipped bludgeon.

I left the consultation and called my plastic surgeon to ask if it would be safe for my newly grown boobs to get fried. *Would they slide off of my body?* He told me that since I'd already had reconstructive surgery and healed from it, most of the potential pitfalls would not be an issue for me. However, I would be at risk for capsular contraction: where the muscle around the implant tightens and starts to mess things up. He assured me he would be there to monitor and follow me through this. I trusted him and was relieved after speaking with him.

After much consideration and prayer, I decided to move forward with radiation. It was not an easy decision to willingly walk back into the fire, but I wanted to live knowing I had done everything within my power to fight back. I beckoned every morsel of courage within me and worked on assembling them into some form of a patchwork quilt.

Monday, March 12, 2018, I went to the hospital for my CT scan. After the mapping was completed, I would have to go in every single Monday through Friday for 25 days. On the day of the CT scan, they gave me a reusable wristband. I thought it was clever, but it also annoyed me. It was like I became emotionally branded and trapped with a shackle that tied me to cancer *again*. I decided that I'd refer to this wristband as jewelry instead, and each day I joked with the ladies at the counter and asked them to return my tennis bracelet to the safe.

They called me back for my scan, and I entered a room at the end of the hall. There was a table and a giant intimidating machine that would scan and circle around me. I got undressed from the waist up, put on a gown, climbed on the table, and laid face up. I was on the verge of tears but had to remain perfectly still. The nurses, both empathetic and kind, placed a bean bag like pillow beneath my head and molded it to my body. This was to ensure that I lay in the same exact position each and every day of treatment. To further aid in alignment, they drew three blue markings on me and covered them with tape.

Then, I had to reach up over my head and hold onto two vertical poles. Some wiring was placed over my right breast, and then the nurses left the room. I closed my eyes and ran my patchwork courage quilt through my mind to keep from crying. That is of course, until I was done and was handed my appointment card with 25 dates and times scheduled on it. The tears raced out; and although I knew it was okay, I felt like an idiot all the same.

It would take about a week or so to create the mapping from the CT scan, so my first radiation appointment was scheduled for Thursday March 22, 2018, the day after my birthday. *Happy Birthday to me; I get radiation therapy.*

I did my best in the interim to live in the moment and enjoy things. I stuffed nearly 230 Easter eggs for an annual egg hunt that we hosted at my house and made party preparations. I continued running; and I went out for a lady's night with a group of friends. I snuggled and read to my girls, planned snacks and goodies for their school Easter parties, and kept up with the normal day-to-day routines.

My good friend, Tonya, did a photoshoot for me on my birthday. We decided that if my birthday and radiation were in the same week, we'd be silly and eat cake despite the looming terror.

I decided to motivate myself with a little countdown chain. I color coordinated the links by week and hung the chain across my mantle. Each day, I would celebrate by ripping off a link. *I could do this.*

I went for a run early in the morning to try and shake away my nerves. Radiation was scheduled for 11:15 a.m., so I had some time to kill. While listening to the rhythm of my feet hitting the pavement and

Fig. 24. Joyce celebrating her birthday the day before radiation on March 21, 2018.
Photographs by Tonya Perry.

feeling the air fill up my lungs, I gave myself another pep talk. *You've got this, Joyce. Twenty-five days is all. There will be no needles or scalpels of any kind. The machine will just circle around you. Another hurdle is all.*

I wanted to hear the sound of hope ringing throughout my journey; I needed to cling to hope, to believe, to keep faith. I wondered about the bell at the cancer institute. I had already rung that damn bell, yet here I was facing treatment again. *Should I have not rung it before? Would I ring it again after radiation was over? When would I REALLY be done?* I reminded myself that hope wasn't at the end; it was along the way. It was not the ending of this trial in my life that held the monopoly on hope. So, yeah—I would ring that bell again at the end of radiation. However, I would celebrate much more than that. I'd celebrate hope by ringing several of my own bells that I'd placed on my mantle *every day* of treatment.

As I entered the radiation wing later that morning, I saw a computer screen with an image of bones displayed...*my* bones.

Fig. 25. Door that led to the radiation room at the cancer institute.

I walked over to the counter by the computer screen to sign a permission form (though this was not a field trip that I was excited about). My eyes couldn't help but study those bones. Those were my ribs, my vertebrae, and my clavicles. My life, the fragility of my own mortality, the true stakes at hand all suddenly flashed to the forefront of my mind.

Over to my right was a giant door, about five inches thick. I was soon ushered through this intimidating entry into the radiation room itself. I heard music playing as I rounded a darkened hall and saw green laser beams throughout the room. I wasn't about to play laser tag, though.

Instead, I was going to be locked behind this gigantic door by myself with radiation penetrating my body. I started to shake, partly because I was freezing to death. I climbed onto the table in the center of the room and was draped with a sheet. I laid on my back and recognized the bean bag mold beneath my head. My knees were propped up with a mold of their own, and I had to reach up over my head and grab ahold of two poles again.

I was shaking so much that the nurses got me a warm toasty blanket to drape over my body. It felt like a giant hug. I was glad that they had music playing; it helped my mind focus on something other than the machine circling me. Although I remained still, I was mentally frantic. I prayed, "Dear God, please help me find courage." Almost immediately, the song playing in the background somehow became a focal point and all I heard were the lines from Journey: "Don't stop believing. Hold on to that feeling" (Journey 1981). The rest of the song faded into the background once more, but those lines looped over and over again in my mind.

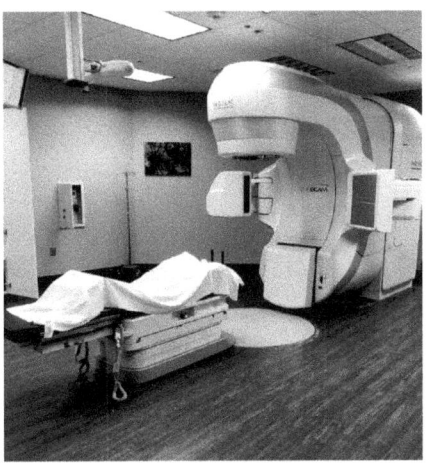

Fig. 26. Radiation machine March and April 2018

One of the other treatment days I was sitting in the waiting room, and an older gentleman was talking with a woman in a pink blazer. I overheard him say that if he made it to 92, then it was God's will; and if he didn't, then that was His will too. My nose signaled its "get ready I sense tears coming" tingle, and sure enough, tears creeped out of my eyes. It was a simple statement—one I had said myself. It just reminded me of my own goal: 95. Yet, I knew it was out of my hands.

When I was in the home stretch and only had a few more treatments remaining, my skin became tender and pink. Then,

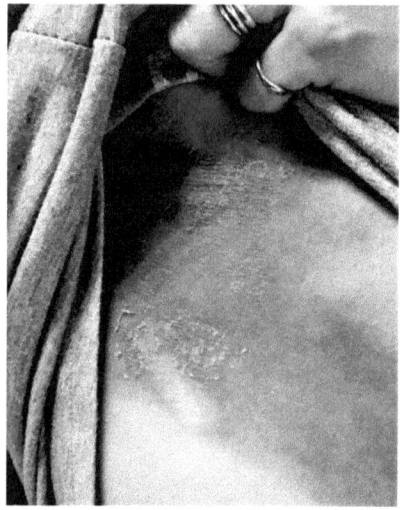

blisters began to form under my arm and beneath the curvature of my breast. My skin turned dark, almost purple, and it began to rip off of me layer by layer: even more of me sacrificed in the name of cancer. My skin was raw and painful; *crispy* is how one radiation patient described it. Whenever I reached for something, my burned flesh would pull and ache,

Fig. 27. My skin darkening after radiation in April 2018

ripping apart any mends that my body had attempted to conjure. However, I was almost done. There was light at the end of this tunnel.

The WTOC news station had gotten wind of my story and wanted to follow me through to the end. So, with my permission, they met me down at the cancer institute on my last day of treatment. With Bryan holding my hand, we walked down the corridors to the machine. After treatment, I grabbed a hold of the string beneath the bell once again. My radiation oncologist, Bryan, the news, and other cancer patients were all there applauding and cheering when the bell rang its sweet sound of hope once more. I did it! I had done every treatment possible for my cancer, and I had no regrets.

I picked my children up from school, and we met our friends at the playground to share a delicious, celebratory cookie cake. Each child also got a pink wristlet with bells on it to shake like crazy.

Token of Courage: Do the Next Right Thing

Fig. 28. Ringing the bell at the cancer institute after completion of radiation therapy

In *Frozen II*, Kristen Bell, who plays Anna, sings "The Next Right Thing," written by Kristen Anderson Lopez and Robert Lopez (2019). Anna slips into a darkened depression, feeling like she's lost all hope while grieving for a loss that leaves her feeling weak and unable to rise. *I know that grief! I know that floor! I know that darkness!* I have felt that cold, unforgiving floor, not knowing if I had the strength to rise. The lyrics coupled with the imagery from the movie itself are together chillingly similar to my emotional experience with cancer. Anna slowly finds her feet beneath her, all while singing about how all she can ask of herself in that moment is to do the next right thing. She inches her way forward, singing:

I won't look too far ahead
It's too much for me to take
But break it down to this next breath, this next step
This next choice is one that I can make

When darkness pulls you down, and you truly have no idea how you can possibly take any more, when you're at your limit, ready to wave that white flag, take Anna's advice for courage token #15, and as Anna sings, "Just do the next right thing. Take a step, step again."

Chapter 16

The Aftershocks

Nugget of Knowledge:

We often associate PTSD with war veterans; however, anyone who has experienced a trauma of any kind (sexual assault, natural disaster, violence, or a medical trauma) is at risk. PTSD is not caused by everyday stress, rather it is a mental health disorder caused by experiencing or witnessing a trauma where one was exposed to actual or threatened serious injury or death; and it requires a diagnosis from a licensed clinician (Posttraumatic stress disorder 2020).

The article, *PTSD and DSM-5*, written by the National Center for PTSD with the U.S. Department of Veteran Affairs summarizes the eight criteria (criterion A-H) for a PTSD diagnosis. The first (criterion A) requires that the person has been exposed to a traumatic event. The second requires that they continually re-experience the traumatic event either through flashbacks, nightmares, or unwanted memories; and the third criterion requires some level of avoidance, either avoiding the emotion associated with the event or physical triggers of the event itself (National Center for PTSD 2018).

Criterion D requires any two of the following negative alterations in cognition and mood: inability to recall parts of the trauma; negative thoughts about oneself or the world (ex: the world is no longer safe); misdirected blame; negative affect; loss of interest in activities; feeling isolated; or difficulty experiencing positive affect. Criterion E for PTSD also requires two of the following arousal and reactivity symptoms: irritability and aggression; risky behavior; hypervigilance; heightened startle reaction; difficulty concentrating; or trouble sleeping (National Center for PTSD 2018). In regards to breast cancer, this might for example be seen as: *my bones ache I probably have a bone met.*

The last three criteria (F, G, and H) for a PTSD diagnosis state that the symptoms have to last for over a month and create distress, and other causalities such as medications or substance abuse must be ruled out (National Center for PTSD 2018). All eight criteria must be met for a PTSD diagnosis.

PTSD essentially changes the brain; it's an injury that needs time and attention in order to heal. It *can* heal; but that won't happen if you ignore it. You wouldn't tell someone who broke their leg to shake it off and be okay already, nor would you feel shameful and try to deny breaking your own leg. No. *I broke my damn leg. It hurts. I'm doing "this" so it can heal.* We ought to give ourselves just as much grace when it comes to a brain injury such as PTSD: *"That" happened; I'm experiencing "this"; and I'm seeking treatment (without shame) so that I can heal… because I am worth it.*

PTSD is not something you can simply will yourself to get over; it requires processing through the trauma, learning to cope with triggers, finding new ways to feel safe in the world, and recognizing and reframing the trauma. We don't have to value and appreciate the terrible event that happened to us, but we can look for ways to bring good from our traumas and/or ways that we can personally grow stronger (Williams 2019, Episode 13). Therapy can help you experience this post-traumatic growth. In *Daring Greatly*, Brené Brown writes, "Only when we're brave enough to explore the darkness will we discover the infinite power of our light" (2012, 60).

Personal Voyage

I knew I couldn't undo my past, and I was determined to find a way to fold it in as part of my being and move on with life. But dang, knowing that and then actually doing that were not on the same playing field; my initial instinct was to run!

Criterion B: Intrusive thoughts and re-experiencing trauma. One afternoon, I settled into a hot shower and allowed myself to feel; my together-exterior finally caught up with my insides, and I fell to the floor…again. I was angry and crying; I slammed my hands against the shower wall, and pulled my knees into my chest as I crouched by the drain and felt the water beat on my back. I began to see the MRI, the hospital, the drains, and the scars; I relived the recoveries, the heartbreak, and the fear. EVERYTHING attacked me at once. I relived it again, and again, and again. I felt the physical and emotional pain of surgery, the knives, the dried blood and glue covering my disfigurement, chemo, needles, my burnt flesh…you name it, it came up and flattened me. I even caught myself frantically trying to back up in the shower stall away from the perceived attack. *If I moved…if I ran…it couldn't reach me (or so the panic-stricken, trauma brain reasoned).*

One day I was called into the lab to get my blood checked for "tumor markers." Tears uncontrollably welled in my eyes; and as I tried to shake them, to change the thoughts in my mind, they flowed incessantly like a river down my cheeks. I signed in at the front and felt the weight of my name tag. It was a stupid fucking sticker, but it weighed a ton and anchored me to cancer. The lab tech jabbed my finger with a needle and squeezed the blood out. I looked around at all of the other sick patients who were queued up for chemo. *Why was I the one crying?* I was done! I have no right to lose it in front of these people. I had no right to lose it at all!

I couldn't seem to explain what was happening. Words failed me. My thoughts were trapped in my brain, and I couldn't get the gears to spin fast enough to make any sense to anybody. It only added to my growing sense of isolation. I somehow managed to communicate "brain fog" and "emotional disaster." The lab tech told me it was to be expected. My body had just been assaulted mentally and physically, at every angle possible, and in a relatively short period of time.

Criterion C: Avoidance. I was afraid to feel…to be reminded of my trauma, so I played a skilled game of 'whack-a-mole' whenever my emotions began to bubble. I didn't want to deal with them. I wanted to numb, but the ignored emotions grew. They scurried in all sorts of directions like pissed off fire ants and bit the fuck out of me everywhere they moved! I tried to shake them off my exterior and shove them back inside quickly, hidden from view. I knew I'd have to address them, but I told myself it wasn't the right time…(*it was never the right time*).

I filled my days with distractions in efforts to make it to my evening glass of wine. Exactly how soon was too soon to call it evening? A glass of red wine was good for the heart anyhow, right? Yet, despite that logic, I didn't want to need anything. That was a path I wanted to avoid. Although I made a choice to pump the brakes and proceed responsibly, I could very easily see how people could choose differently, especially when faced with overwhelming and unwanted emotions. Eventually, I welcomed sleep as my escape hatch. Only, it became a cruel joke when I started having nightmares.

Criterion D: Negative thoughts or feelings. I harbored sadness, grief, fear of the possibility of recurrence (what if a slippery bastard evaded the chemo?), and anger at the whole damn thing. Sweet conversations with my kids even made me tear up with the thought of my mortality. *What if I had died? I could have missed this!* Then a twinge of guilt began to rise accompanying the fear that I *could* have left my children motherless. Logically, I knew that I was strong; I had faced the unthinkable in order to live, to be there with my children. However, post-trauma, I assigned myself blame and guilt for what could have been.

I thought about my children and how I wanted to protect them from pain, which in turn made me empathize with my mother. I'd much rather be the patient than the mother of the patient, especially when you knew there wasn't a damn thing you could do to wipe away their pain. That would be excruciating for any parent, yet I did that to my mom. Although cancer was not my fault, I blamed myself all the same for the heartache I caused.

I also thought about Bryan and how difficult it must have been for him too…how powerless he must have felt when a life-threatening disease weaved its way into our lives. He'd promised to love, honor, and cherish me…in sickness and in health. He wanted to protect me, but he couldn't defend me from cancer's reach or shield me from its terror—no one could. He was just as powerless as the rest of us. How infuriating that must have been for him. To watch a loved one struggle and be unable to bear any part of that load for them must have been insufferable. *I could have left my husband before old age. We had plans to grow old together. What if I left him alone to raise our girls without their mother? How could I do this to him? To my whole family?*

I expected immense relief to accompany survivorship…and I was relieved, don't get me wrong. I was joyful and grateful, but this was only part of what I felt. *Why was my life spared? How was I lucky enough to find it early and to fight it in time, when others weren't?* It didn't seem fair. *Why was I granted time when the next person wasn't?* Fused together were gratitude and guilt, wound together so tightly they couldn't be pulled apart. Then, I felt ashamed and guilty once more for feeling anything other than gratitude for the gift that I had just received.

I started to think about all of the people I knew who had fought cancer. Some were old, some young; there were men, women, and children. Some survived and others didn't. Some were given months to live; others were given a clean bill of health only to have it reoccur later. Cancer didn't discriminate.

I thought about life and how it came and how it went—often unexpectedly. I thought about how each one of us mattered. We all set ripples into motion, etched our words into the wind, and shaped the world just a little bit while we breathed upon it. We all had value. So why was I granted life when the next person who had done everything right was not?

Criterion E: Trauma related arousal and reactivity. I had survived, so why did I feel like I couldn't do this anymore? Anger pumped through my veins, and I wanted to throw my computer across the room, slam doors, or hit something! My fingers in their fury locked into fists around the tiny strands of hair that I had grown. I fought against my rage through my uncontrollable sobbing and forced my fists to open. However, I was still angry. My fists opened with a stiffness known only to anger: anger at

166

cancer, anger at what it took, anger at my emotional volatility, anger for not having put it behind me, for not being enough, and anger for what cancer might do if it came back.

Criterion E: Hypervigilance. My bones ached, so naturally my mind raced to thoughts of bone mets. Exhaustion would hit, and I'd panic that I had a recurrence. I later felt a tiny, new lump on the side where I once had cancer. *Was this it? Had my cancer returned?* (Later, a biopsy was performed and concluded that it was benign). However, every bump and bruise seemed to trigger the fear of *what-if.*

*   *   *

It snowed in early January; it really snowed! In Coastal Georgia, we got three to four inches! Our driveway was one of the very few hills in the county, so anybody within walking distance came to go sledding. We used boogie boards and pool toys, whatever we could find. We even put three kids in a baby pool and sent that thing sailing down the driveway. We laughed, we played…we had a ball. We made snow angels and snowmen, had snowball fights and hot chocolate. It was a perfectly timed and welcomed distraction.

I started running again. I couldn't go far and Lord knew I hurt afterwards, but I was proud of my two miles. It felt good to be able to do something that had been taken away from me. I scheduled lunches and coffees with friends; I took the girls on play dates and filled every moment with something for me to think of aside from cancer.

This journey had changed me in ways that I was still discovering. I was learning how to function physically and emotionally with a foreign newness that I didn't yet understand. Ashley reminded me that it was normal to experience unexpected emotions after a great loss or suffering. I needed to give myself time to process through what had happened and what I was feeling in the aftermath.

I had holes on my abdomen, a belly button that no longer mirrored my original, two prostheses for breasts that could no longer feel the sensation of my own touch, and a mental image of the emptiness inside me from where my organs were once housed. I had a complex relationship with the renovations that pieced together my new body. I both loved them for what they saved me from and hated them for what I had to be saved from.

Nevertheless, this body still belonged to my mind, to my spirit, to my soul; and I felt comfort in knowing that it was still me. I was still me despite what had been lost. I *owned* this body…complete with every imperfection that my eyes and mind could scrutinize. I would find a way to come to peace with that.

Token of Courage: It's Okay to Float

Floating on your back is the very first thing that we teach our children when they're learning to swim. If they fall in the deep end of the pool, or if they get exhausted and start to panic, we teach them to roll over onto their backs to float. It doesn't mean that they're done with the swim altogether (they still have to make it to the pool's edge), and it doesn't mean that they're giving up either. They're simply taking a moment to catch their breath, re-strategize, and regain some strength to tackle their next stroke.

When I felt like I was in over my head, fatigued, and likely to drown at any moment, Ashley asked me, "In these moments, what is wrong with rolling onto your back to float?" *Genius!* Metaphor is my language. Floating is taking a moment to just be. Floating could look different from one person to the next depending on them and their situation. Sometimes it is just breathing, taking long deep breaths and focusing on that one thing alone. It could be taking a hot shower and letting the beads of water wash the worries off your back, even if it is only for the duration of the shower. It could be through prayer, or exercise, or sipping a hot cup of coffee, feeling the transfer of heat from the mug to your body. It could be journaling or painting or sitting alone for a moment and listening to music, allowing yourself to feel whatever emotions stirred and let them be.

So, when you feel like you're drowning, take a moment to roll onto your back and float. There's no rush. Catch your breath, rest, and gather yourself for the next leg of the journey.

Chapter 17

Piecing it Together

Nugget of Knowledge

We may wonder when we can call our journeys over; or at what point can we actually claim "Happily Ever After?" We may expect to neatly wrap up our stories with exquisite bows once we've crossed that threshold past treatment. *Tada! Nailed it!* However, it doesn't work that way. Life is a journey; and we will continue to struggle, to celebrate, to laugh, to cry, to exceed our goals, and to fall short. This process doesn't stop when our treatments stop.

I decided to put together a free, research-based resilience curriculum for my fellow pink ladies. I spent months diving into literature and curriculum planning. The research showed that there were, what I call, *Six Pillars to Resilience*; and when you strengthen each one, you in turn strengthen your overall ability to move past your trauma. These six pillars are: *Self-care and Compassion; Support and Connection; Positive Affect; Healthy Coping Strategies; Finding Purpose; and Practicing Mindfulness.*

There are concrete things that we can do to rewire our brains for resilience, but first it's helpful to understand how our brains work in processing stress and trauma in the first place. There are three main parts of the brain. The cerebral cortex is in charge of logic and reason; the limbic brain is in charge of emotions and feelings; and the "reptilian brain" (located at the base of your brain stem) is responsible for basic survival instincts, specifically that infamous fight-flight response to danger. Your amygdala rests in the limbic brain and can be thought of as your giant fire alarm; it goes off when fear is experienced to activate your body's response.

On any given hunky-dory day, the limbic brain and cerebral cortex can communicate just fine. However, when the alarm bell (aka the amygdala) sounds, it yanks the reins away from our logical/reasoning brain and sends control to our reptilian brain. Our cortisol increases, we may begin rapid breathing or sweating, and we gear up to self-protect: to fight or to flight. Again, our bodies are like this by design, to protect us in times of great danger.

After a traumatic experience, the amygdala actually grows, which can explain the hypervigilance we experience … the constant feeling of being on edge, or waiting for the next shoe to drop, so to speak. Furthermore, our ability to access the logical/reasoning part of our brain gets hindered because the alarm keeps giving the reins to "fight-or-flight." Mindfulness, on the other hand, can actually shrink the amygdala and increase access to the cerebral cortex (The Great Courses 2019).

Siegel and Bryson (2011) say in *The Whole-Brain Child*, "Experience is what molds our brain…actually changing the physical structure of it" (7). This is critical because it gives us a bit of control back. You see, your brain is made of a bunch of cells called neurons. Siegel and Bryson say that neurons that fire together wire together, and there are about 100,000 neurons, each with about 10,000 pathways to other neurons. *That's a lot of pathways!*

We can use our understanding of how the brain works to our advantage. Knowing that experiences are what connect neurons and wire pathways, we can essentially rewire our brains for resilience by creating NEW experiences—and thus new pathways. This ability to rewire our brains is called neuroplasticity, and if we can align this with our understanding of resilience, then we are setting ourselves up for success.

The first of the Six Pillars to Resilience is *Self-Care and Compassion*; and it relates with both our physical resilience and our emotional/mental resilience. The online article, Resilience (2020), in Psychology Today shares the importance of getting adequate sleep, eating a healthy diet, staying hydrated, exercising, and practicing self-care. Birkholm even adds in her resilience curriculum with The Great Courses (2019) that exercising with a group increases accountability and support; and yoga itself touches on the practice of mindfulness and emotional/mental well-being while simultaneously building your physical strength. In regards to self-care and compassion with our emotional resilience, it ultimately involves our ability to radically accept our emotions.

How on earth do we get to this acceptance? Well, for all of my type A outliners who want a step-by-step guideline, here is my best crack at it.

Step 1: Recognize the sensations you're feeling and name them (McKay, Wood, and Brantley 2007).

Step 2: Practice mindful breathing. This will help reconnect your emotional brain to your logical/reasoning part of your brain, ultimately paving the way for us to better tend to those emotional wounds. There are several techniques for mindful breathing … a simple Google search will lead you right to them. One technique is "spiral breathing." Here you trace (either in the air or on paper) a spiral ... moving your finger clockwise while you inhale and counterclockwise while you exhale.

Step 3: Practice some healthy coping strategies. This is so huge that it's actually one of its own pillars to resilience.

The second pillar to resilience is *Support and Connection*. It's important to remember that you are not alone... your journey may be 100% unique to you, but you don't have to do it alone. Lean in to your support network, practice authenticity, and know that it is okay to fall to pieces. When we share our experiences with our support system, it decreases depression and normalizes our humanity. Friends, family, other survivors, support groups, and therapists can all be part of this support and connection network.

Positive Affect—the third pillar to resilience—is when we are able to experience positive emotions and hold relatively positive views on the world. Mejia-Downs (2017) explains that MRIs show different parts of the brain being used when we consider our positive experiences compared to thinking about our negative ones. You can work towards rewiring the brain and cultivating more resilience when you focus on counteracting negative thought cycles with positive ones (Resilience, 2020).

Doing good for others and showing gratitude for what you have are two ways that Mejia-Downs says that this can be done (2017). Writing three positive things from the day in a gratitude journal is a great practice. So, if I had an emotionally draining cancer-fighting day, and I fell to pieces boohooing in the lobby (been there), a positive might still be: *I chose to go to the doctor today. It may have been hard and I may have cried my eyes out, but I did it and I am that much closer to being done with this step.*

Mejia-Downs (2017) explains how humor and optimism can increase one's positive affect, and thus build resilience as well. According to her, humor can be stimulated by watching comedies or reading a joke of the day; you could also share funny memes or video clips with friends. She says that "optimism is future oriented; it is the hope and confidence that everything will work out—so it helps one move forward."

She challenges you to insert a positive thought about a situation whenever a negative experience or thought rises (Mejia-Downs 2017). So, for example, if a friend says something hurtful like, "Oh, I know someone who had cancer…they died from it," or if they minimize your fears by saying, "You're going to be fine, don't worry," you can insert a positive thought such as, "My friend loves me and is just trying to connect with me." Losing my hair to chemo was incredibly traumatic, and (as crazy as it may sound) it was in some ways harder than losing my breasts. Knowing that my hair was falling out was a negative thought/experience; however, I could spin it by saying, "Each strand that falls out is me taking one step closer to having this journey behind me."

Healthy Coping Strategies is the fourth pillar to resilience (and the third step to acceptance). Healthy coping refers to positive ways to handle stress when it arrives. Maybe you go for a run, do yoga or some other form of physical activity, practice mindfulness, listen to music, burn essential oils, take deep breaths, take a bubble bath … whatever works for you. You work to let go of what you can't control and turn your efforts to focusing on what you can. The trick here is to avoid unhealthy numbing strategies such as excessive drinking, sleeping, or keeping so busy that you never slow down long enough to feel. Therapy can most definitely help with finding strategies and processing through emotions in a safe/healthy manner.

The fifth pillar to resilience is *Finding Purpose*. Traumas happen, adversity hits, we fall, we bleed, we ache. But, if we can find ways to use our experiences to push forward with purpose and conviction, then we help cultivate that resilience even further. Ask yourself, what do you care about? What is it that motivates and inspires you? When adversity strikes, we can either let it destroy us or, in the process of busting us open, let it help us find our true authentic selves. In the Great Courses class on *The Foundation of Resilience*, Birkholm says that we can use our trials to reunite ourselves with our core values; and our core values, she says, are the very "Bedrock of Resilience" (The Great Courses 2019). What are the must-have values that you live by? These are the values that give your life meaning and are northern stars to finding your purpose. Your purpose can be related to your trauma or completely unrelated to it too; the point is that you *use your experiences* to reunite yourself with these values and find purpose.

The sixth pillar to resilience is *Mindfulness*, which we discussed in a previous chapter. The point here is that you work on being present in the now, being mindfully aware of your thoughts, feelings, and sensations…recognizing their life cycle, and not judging them…living in the moment. You can use your imagination to practice bringing your attention to an emotion, noticing its strength, refraining from turning from it, observing it until it changes. You can imagine a wave of emotions rolling in and then receding (McKay, Wood, and Brantley 2007).

Personal Voyage

I had a miscarriage prior to my pregnancy with my eldest, Leona; and, like many other women, I battled fears over things that I clearly could not control. Even though I knew my miscarriage wasn't my fault, there wasn't anything I could have done, and that "these things happen," I felt powerless in my inability to protect my baby from harm. The pain and grief that accompanied that loss were real; and when I became pregnant again, this time with Leona, I couldn't wait to hold my child in my arms. I reasoned that if I could only get past the pregnancy and have my little girl nestled down safe and snug in my arms, *then* I could have the power and control to protect her from the world around us.

The funny thing was, when I held her in my arms for the first time, the worry didn't dissipate. It simply changed forms. When I held that sweet little girl in my arms and became a mom for the first time, I wanted more than anything to protect her from harm, to shield her from any and all heartache and pain in the world.

The truth is, however, there is pain in this world. Sadness and grief accompany each of us, whether we like it or not. They are real emotions, part of the human experience. I can't protect my children from all the hurt and heartache their paths in life will bring. The best I can hope for is to teach them how to handle discomfort and pain when things go awry. We cannot control all the events in our lives, but we can control our perspective and our actions. We can model, practice, and teach resilience.

Heartache and pain hit my little girl with a mean-girl comment from school one day, and I wasn't able to prevent it, to shield her from it. I knew things were going to come up in her life that she was going to have to learn how to handle. However, after having experienced my fair share of mean-girl comments in my youth, I knew that pain. It sucked, and my heart ached for her all the same. It reminded me of what Dr. Seuss (1990) wrote in *Oh the Places You'll Go*:

There's fun to be done!
There are points to be scored. There are games to be won.
And the magical things you can do with that ball
will make you the winning-est winner of all.
Fame! You'll be famous as famous can be,
With the whole wide world watching you win on TV.
Except when they don't.
Because, sometimes they won't.
I'm afraid that *some*times
you'll play lonely games too.
Games you can't win
'cause you'll play against you.

Seuss nailed it. It is undeniably true. When we stop to examine our own lives, victory and defeat are a whole packaged deal. No human being is immune from the fractures and falls that life brings our way.

A similar fear of failure surfaced when one of my littles was learning to ride her bike. She had fallen off a few times and scraped her knees; big tears would roll down her cheeks, and she no longer wanted to ride. We talked a lot about failure, and how it wasn't always a bad thing; it built determination and perseverance. The motto, "We can do hard things" became a frequently used household expression. Sure enough, she learned to ride. It was hard, and it hurt, but when she fell, she picked herself up, brushed herself off, and tried again.

When these moments come—and they inevitably will—you don't need to have all the answers for how to move past them. You just need to take a deep breath and believe that you will, because you will. Time and time again, you will.

I got a healthy lesson early on in my cancer-fighting journey that there would be large and small trials in our lives, but no matter the size, they both required resilience. For me, there was the *big one*: fighting for my life, for my ability to be present in my children's lives as they grew. And then, there were buttons: the seemingly trivial problems that caused heartache all the same.

I want my children to learn resilience for the "button" moments as well as the life-altering ones. Whether it's emotional pain that accompanies mean-girl exclusion at school or a bigger life-altering moment such as the death of a loved one, a traumatic event, or a life-threatening illness, we can rise up again. We are not immune from pain (large or small), but we are capable of moving through that pain and emerging as a stronger, wiser version of ourselves.

I don't want my children to experience adversity one day, look back at this book, and hear nothing but sunshine and rainbows. I want them to hear it all. I want them to hear my pain *and* my joy, and I want them to know that they will experience them both too. Love yourself through it all; find your feet beneath you once more; and take your next step forward.

*   *   *

I was driving around town during one of the darkest periods of my journey—exhausted, weary, weak, and woeful with the lack of control in my life—especially with the fear of my mortality center stage. I just didn't think I could do it anymore, so I put my hands together and prayed real hard for guidance, for help, for some level of control. That's when Randy Travis's song, "Three Wooden Crosses," came across the air. I let the lines, "I guess it's not what you take when you leave this world behind you, it's what you leave behind you when you go" seep in (2002). There's so much wisdom in that. *What did I want to leave behind?* I couldn't control when my time came; however, I could control what I left behind.

Almost immediately, a beautiful image of snow accompanying a hope-filled metaphor came to me. "If acts of kindness are unique like snowflakes, then when we increase these acts, we get to see the snow." *That's it!* I wanted to leave behind that metaphorical snow, and that started with snowflakes. Each and every day that I'm here, I could focus on a "snowflake—on some element of kindness."

In April 2018, one of my cancer-fighting friends asked if I'd consider participating in a walk with her. I was thrilled to take part in something greater than myself, and I was especially proud of my friend who was driven to advocate for early detection and create something amazing from her own trials.

Miranda Lambert (2016) sings, "I'm bent, but I'm not broken. I'm stronger than I feel...I'm the keeper of the flame, the teller of the story...for the ones that came before me, for the little pilot lights waiting to ignite, like fireflies in the rain." My friend commented on how she loved that it was our collective stories and experiences that united us and gave comfort. I added that together we would weather this storm: our own storms and the greater challenge of finding a cure. It would take us all coming together to move these mountains, but the more we united, the brighter the light would shine. I wanted that lighthouse to radiate light so brightly that no "little pilot lights waiting to ignite, like fireflies in the rain" felt alone while weathering their storms.

Passion and purpose fueled me with strength and rejuvenation. I soon started a website www.togetherweweather.org, where I included educational and inspirational support, along with resources and their hyperlinks. I created a podcast to empower women, their support networks, and our communities even further. I interviewed breast surgeons, radiation oncologists, plastic surgeons, genetic counselors, therapists, authors, medical tattoo artists, survivors, and more.

I continued to peer-mentor, to advocate and volunteer, and to connect local patients with resources available in our areas. I spoke with women on both an individual and group basis. During the COVID-19 pandemic, I helped organize informational and support webinars for breast cancer patients and survivors to have while quarantined; and I dove into the literature, designed, and produced a free, research-based curriculum for breast cancer patients.

I partnered up with Dr. Elisabeth Counselman-Carpenter, PhD, LCSW, at Adelphi University, to investigate patient views on the psychosocial implications of a breast cancer diagnosis and mental health support. Our goal is to educate patients, providers, clinicians, and community members with IRB research studies and to further programs based on peer-reviewed research.

In April 2022, I began the steps to incorporate Keepers of the Flame® and to file for nonprofit in efforts to continue the mission. Carrie Mott (survivor, and one of my personal "lighthouses"), Jen Davis (NP – women's health; survivorship and high-risk program coordinator), Ashley Moore (LMFT), and Vanessa Brink (NP – medical oncology) agreed to serve as the first Board of Directors for Keepers of the Flame® Foundation, Inc. Through community partnerships, grants, and public support, our nonprofit grew exponentially, and we were able to launch programs that supported local patients. We added transportation and hardship assistance, Empowerment Photography sessions, and with a grant from Brother's Brother Foundation, we were able to launch a Financial Assistance to Counseling program.

Through all these efforts, I rose to my feet, hung onto my courage and resilience, and pushed past my barriers with purpose and conviction. I wanted my girls to inherit a world of cancer care even better and more advanced than the one I lived in. I wanted the world to look back at the radiation table I used and think that it was archaic; and I wanted emotional healing, as a universal and normal part of the journey, to be talked about openly and freely at family dinner tables.

My life is *still* a journey; and with that comes more stumbles and more falls...alongside more hope, more courage, and more strength. You may hear me bawling my eyes out on some random Tuesday, but then again, I might be dancing in my kitchen on Wednesday. I will journey onward, and so will you.

Token of Courage: You Have What it Takes

Throughout my journey, I collected little tokens of courage that together painted a mural for courage in its entirety. As I assembled these puzzle pieces, I began to get a better idea of how we can move through our adversities and stand as stronger individuals on the other side.

Just like when you work a real puzzle and begin to conceptualize the big picture right before you put in the final pieces, the same holds true with finding courage. Courage doesn't take one form or come to us in one single moment. Rather, it's the collection of these lessons, of these moments in our own lives where we can hear its truth and piece it together for ourselves. So, when adversity comes banging on your own door, screaming and howling at you in the middle of your night, remember that you *do* have courage. Put it together one piece at a time!

I'd painstakingly learned these themes within my journey; and after having been forced to lean on them myself and trust in their validity when life knocked me down again, they were what helped me rise once more. They grabbed my hand and helped to lift me up from that callous, unforgiving pavement. I wasn't without abrasions, bruises, and lacerations from the fall itself, and standing to my feet again was sure as hell one of the most difficult things I have ever done. However, it was easier when I trusted that it *could* be done.

Accept all of yourself. Let go of what you can't control and shift your attention to that which you can. Make decisions with the information available to you at the time, and do the best you can. Love yourself. Get back up and sculpt goodness from those shadows. Know that YOU are enough. Emotional scars are just as real as the physical ones. You don't need to know how to move forward, you just need to believe that you will. Ask for help. You matter. You DO have courage; we all do.

We can be courageous and sail through uncertainty, persevere from tragedy, and shape our world for the better with our newly found perspective and strength. These opportunities are afforded to us all, not just a select few.

Admiral William McRaven gave a speech in August 2017. He spoke about life and perseverance by using the navy seal night swim and training as a metaphor. He said:

…if a shark begins to circle your position, stand your ground. Do not swim away. Do not act afraid. And if a shark, hungry for a midnight snack, darts towards you, then summon up all your strength and punch him in the snout; and he will turn and swim away. There are a lot of sharks in the world. If you hope to complete the swim, you will have to deal with them. So, if you want to change the world, don't back down from the sharks…if I have learned anything in my time traveling the world, it is the power of hope. One person can change the world by giving people hope…know that life is not fair and that you will fail often. But, if you take some risks, step up when the times are the toughest, face down the bullies, lift up the downtrodden, and never ever give up…if you do these things, the next generation and the generations that follow will live in a world far better than the one we have today.

And what started here, will indeed have changed the world for the better.

I never asked for cancer; and although I have found value in the *new me* and have grown stronger from my trials, if I were given the chance for a do-over, I'm pretty sure I'd say, "Keep that shit the hell away from me!" I still struggle with the emotions that accompany that beast. I am fearful of it coming back again. I am angry and heartbroken that I had to live through such physical and emotional tortures in the first place. However, that is not all that I am. I am determined. I am hopeful. I believe in the power of goodness and the potential residing within each of us. I believe that I will move past my own pain; and I have faith that in being vulnerable with my own ordeal my children and their children's children will learn these things as well. So yes, it is my hope that "what started here, will indeed have changed the world for the better." What started as pain and terror with a cancer diagnosis will somehow help us all in gathering tokens of courage.

About the Author

Joyce Williams grew up a submariner's daughter, moving every three years. She met her husband while running cross country in high school, but she didn't date him until after college when they reconnected with old fashioned letters. Joyce graduated from Furman University with a Biology degree and spent seven years teaching middle and high schoolers before staying home with their two little girls. Joyce serendipitously discovered that she had the BRCA2 mutation, elevating her lifetime risk to 84%. She wasn't sick, never felt a lump, and was years away from the recommended screening age. Yet, at the age of 36, Joyce was diagnosed with invasive ductal carcinoma.

Since treatment, Joyce wanted to normalize the mental health aspect of a diagnosis and help women find the support they needed. She created a podcast interviewing key professionals, taught and produced a free resilience curriculum, and did IRB investigations and peer-reviewed publications with Dr. Elisabeth Counselman-Carpenter on breast cancer patient preferences on psychotherapy.

Joyce is the founder of Keepers of the Flame® Foundation, a 501(c)(3) supporting breast cancer patients physically and emotionally. "If acts of kindness are unique in their own beauty, like snowflakes, then when we increase these acts, we get to see the snow." Joyce is known for teaching about the power of metaphorical snow, how it begins with 'snowflakes', and that in focusing on them, we're able to feel more in control of our lives, find purpose, and make the world better—even through the most difficult times.

Joyce loves spending time with her family, doing yoga, going to the beach, and cheering on her girls at swim meets.

References

American Cancer Society Medical and Editorial Content Team. *Survival Rates for Breast Cancer.* Last modified January 8, 2020. https://www.cancer.org/cancer/breast-cancer/understanding-a-breast-cancer-diagnosis/breast-cancer-survival-rates.html

Bell, Kristen. "The Next Right Thing." By Kristen Anderson-Lopez and Robert Lopez. Recorded ca. 2019. On *Frozen II.* Walt Disney Records, MP3.

Brown, Brené. *Daring Greatly: How the Courage to Be Vulnerable Transforms the Way We Live, Love, Parent, and Lead.* New York, NY: Avery an imprint of Penguin Random House, 2012.

Chilkov, Nalini. "Ten Warning Signs of Ovarian Cancer/ The Silent Killer." Last modified 2025. http://www.integrativecanceranswers.com/ten-warning-signs-of-ovarian-cancer-the-silent-killer/

Counselman-Carpenter, Elizabeth, and Alex Redcay. *Working with Grief & Traumatic Loss: Theory, Practice, Personal Reflection, and Self-care.* San Diego, CA: Cognella, Inc., 2020.

Dorn, Walt, and Mike Mitchell, dirs. *Trolls.* 2016; Glendale, CA: DreamWorks Animation, 2017. DVD.

Fritscher, Lisa. "How to Be Vulnerable: Examples of Vulnerability and How It Can Improve Your Relationships." Last modified November 20, 2023. https://www.verywellmind.com/fear-of-vulnerability-2671820

Journey. "Don't stop believin'." By Jonathan Cain, Steve Perry, and Neal Schon. Recorded ca. 1981. On *Escape*. Columbia Records, CD.

Kendrick, Anna. "Get Back Up Again." By Benj Pasek and Justin Paul. Recorded ca. 2016. On *Trolls*. RCA Records, CD.

Kendrick, Anna, and Justin Timberlake. "True Colors." By Tom Kelly and Billy Steinberg. Recorded ca. 2016. On *Trolls*. RCA Records, CD.

Lambert, Miranda. "Keeper of the Flame." By Natalie Hemby, Miranda Lambert, and Liz Rose. Recorded ca. 2016. On *The Weight of These Wings*. Sony/ATV Music Publishing LLC, Warner/Chappell Music, Inc., and Cypmp, CD.

Docter, Pete, dir. *Inside out*. 2015; Emeryville, CA: Pixar Animation Studios, 2015. DVD.

Leslie, Kate, and Megan Allen. "Health Check: Why Can You Feel Groggy Days After an Operation?" May 17, 2017. https://findanexpert.unimelb.edu.au/news/5575-health-check--why-can-you-feel-groggy-days-after-an-operation%3F

Linehan, Marsha. "Marsha Linehan on Radical

Acceptance." 2019. Video, 0:33. https://byronclinic.
com/marsha-linehan-radical-acceptance/

McKay, Matthew, Jeffrey C. Wood., and Jeffrey Brantley.
*The Dialectical Behavior Therapy Skills Workbook:
Practical DBT Exercises for Learning Mindfulness,
Interpersonal Effectiveness, Emotional Regulation, &
Distress Tolerance.* Oakland, CA: New Harbinger
Publications, Inc., 2007.

McGuinness, Aniela. "Love My Mastectomy: Top 5 Weird
Reasons." September 4, 2015. Video, 6:26. https://
www.youtube.com/watch?v=THykprttD1A

McRaven, William. "If You Want to Change the World,
Start Off by Making Your Bed." August 17, 2017.
Video, 6:00. https://www.bing.com/videos/h?q=speech
+about+making+your+bed&view=detail&mid=8C3E1
BF75937460915248C3E1BF7593746091524&FOR
M=VIRE

Mejia-Downs, Anne. "Resilience: Everyone Has It -
What Will You Do with Yours? *Cardiopulmonary
Physical Therapy Journal,* 28, no. 3 (2017): 93-98.
https://journals.lww.com/cptj/Fulltext/2017/07000/
Resilience__Everyone_Has_It_What_Will_You_Do_
With.3.aspx

National Center for PTSD. "PTSD and DSM-5." Last
modified March 25, 2025. https://www.ptsd.va.gov/
professional/treat/essentials/dsm5_ptsd.asp

"Posttraumatic stress disorder." Traumadissociation.com.

Accessed May 28, 2020. http://traumadissociation. com/ptsd.html.

Redmoon, Ambrose. "No peaceful warriors." *Gnosis,* Fall 1991.

"Resilience." Psychology Today. Accessed June 1, 2020. https://www.psychologytoday.com/us/basics/resilience

Rowling, J.K. *Harry Potter and the Order of the Phoenix.* New York, NY: Scholastic Press, a division of Scholastic Inc, 2003.

Seladi-Schulman, Jill. "What Part of the Brain Controls Emotions?" July 23, 2018. https://www.healthline.com/ health/what-part-of-the-brain-controls-emotions#anger

Settle, Keala, and The Greatest Showman Ensemble. "This is Me." By Benj Pasek and Justin Paul. Recorded ca. 2017. On *The Greatest Showman: Original Motion Picture Soundtrack.* Atlantic Records, CD.

Seuss Geisel, Theodore. *Oh, the Places You'll Go.* New York, NY: Random House, 1990.

Siegel, Daniel J., and Tina P. Bryson. *The Whole-Brain Child: 12 Revolutionary Strategies to Nurture Your Child's Developing Mind.* New York, NY: Delacorte Press, an imprint of The Random House Publishing Group, 2011.

Stevenson, John, and Mark Osborne, dirs. *Kung Fu Panda.* 2008; Glendale, CA: DreamWorks Animation, 2008. DVD.

The Great Courses, dir. *The Foundation of Resilience*. 2019; The Teaching Company, LLC. Online Video Course.

Thuret, Sandrine. "You Can Grow New Brain Cells: Here's How." June 2015. Video, 10:54. https://www.ted.com/talks/sandrine_thuret_you_can_grow_new_brain_cells_here_s_how

Travis, Randy. "Three Wooden Crosses." By Kim Williams and Doug Johnson. Recorded ca. 2002. On *Rise and Shine*. Word Music/Curb, CD.

Williams, Joyce. "Podcast #7: Radiation Oncology with Dr. Michael Hasselle." Keepers of the Flame®. July 17, 2019. https://podcasts.apple.com/us/podcast/keepers-of-the-flame/id1467408440?i=1000444653460

Williams, Joyce. "Podcast #13: Trauma, PTSD, and Breast Cancer with Ashley Moore, MS, LMFT." Keepers of the Flame®. August 28, 2019. https://podcasts.apple.com/us/podcast/keepers-of-the-flame/id1467408440?i=1000447979896

Williams, Joyce. "Podcast #28: High Risk Breast Cancer Clinic - What Does It Mean with Jennifer Davis." Keepers of the Flame®. December 10, 2019. https://podcasts.apple.com/us/podcast/keepers-of-the-flame/id1467408440?i=1000459264925

Williams, Joyce. "Podcast #39: Medical Oncology with Vanessa Brink." Keepers of the Flame®. February 26, 2020. https://podcasts.apple.com/us/podcast/keepers-of-the-flame/id1467408440?i=1000466708370

Williams, Joyce. "Podcast #45: Understanding Pathology with Pathologist Dr. Charles Todd Bruker, M.D." Keepers of the Flame®. April 8, 2020. https://podcasts.apple.com/us/podcast/keepers-of-the-flame/id1467408440?i=100047083772

www.ingramcontent.com/pod-product-compliance
Lightning Source LLC
Chambersburg PA
CBHW051517120626
46551CB00012B/969